D1744864

Therapy with children

A new skill for counsellors

Roger & Christine Day

Brook Creative Therapy

Published by:

Brook Creative Therapy, 16 Burnside, Rugby, Warwickshire CV22 6AX, UK.

Acknowledgments

This book would not have been possible without the hundreds of people from several nations who attended our workshops over the years.

For four years we provided training programmes for therapy with children in various cities around Romania. Many hundreds of psychologists and psychiatrists, as well as other professionals, attended those trainings. They were mainly from Romania but others came from Serbia, Russia and Hungary. Many of them gave excellent feedback in helping to develop further training programmes.

Then for several years in various parts of the British Isles we ran our eight-day training event known as the Postgraduate Certificate in Counselling Children & Families. People gave us good feedback along the way that helped us improve what we were presenting. Although we stopped running this programme on our retirement, other people have successfully offered it under licence from us.

This book contains the revised material from that eight-day course, which itself incorporated material from the first trainings in Romania.

A big thank you to Kathryn Revell for reading the book and giving useful comments.

Thank you to each one of you who have played your part in making this book possible.

Roger & Christine Day
July 2018

Books by Roger & Christine Day available through Amazon's CreateSpace:

Matryoshkas in Therapy: Creative ways to use Russian dolls with clients

Creative Anger Expression

Creative Therapy in the Sand: Using sandtray with clients

Body Awareness: 64 bodywork activities for therapy

Therapeutic Adventure: 64 activities for therapy outdoors

Stories that Heal: 64 creative visualisations for use in therapy

Therapy with Children: A new skill for counsellors

You can discover more about a person in an hour of play than in a year of conversation.
– Plato, Greek philosopher 427–347 BC

Therapy with Children: A new skill for counsellors

About the authors:

Roger Day
Certified Transactional Analyst, Psychotherapist and Play Therapy specialist
For many years Roger was a psychotherapist, trainer and supervisor specialising in children and families. Now retired, he lives with his wife Christine in Rugby, Warwickshire, UK.

Christine Day
European Adult Teaching Certificate, Nursery Nurse Examination Board (NNEB), Diploma in Counselling
Christine is a qualified nursery nurse and counsellor. In addition to raising a family, over the years she has added play and creativity specialisms to her nursery skills as well as considerable training experience.

Roger & Christine Day

Contents

Therapy with Children: A new skill for counsellors

The dream

Our dream started in the early 1990s when we began providing counselling for children and young people. Some of these came from painful situations of domestic violence where what the children had seen and heard had left them traumatised.

'Why don't more counsellors help child clients?' we asked ourselves.

And so emerged our dream: To help raise up many counsellors besides ourselves to meet children's emotional needs before they became adults.

Over the next couple of years we wrote an article on this: *What about the children?* Although it wasn't published at the time, it has been incorporated – virtually as it was written – into the second part of this book's introduction.

Around the turn of the Millennium Roger approached the children's supervision group of which he had been a member for several years. 'What would be needed to help qualified counsellors and psychotherapists to become skilled in working with children and young people as well as adults?' he asked.

After considerable discussion the conclusion was that qualified counsellors and psychotherapists would need a minimum of eight days' specialist training, practical experience and creative supervision to begin working effectively with under-16s.

The dream nearly died when we visited Romania in December 2003 and felt a strong, God-given urge to offer therapy to children there on a full-time basis. Since Romanian dictator Ceauçescu's dramatic downfall and the collapse of communism in December 1989, needy children there had been provided with food, clothes, housing, education and medicine. The one thing missing was any kind of help with their emotions.

Nearly a whole generation had passed since we had seen on our TV screens those shocking images of children suffering in institutional care in Romania. Yet we now realised that children born since communism were still carrying the anger, hurt and trauma of the previous generation.

After time spent in preparation, we moved to Oradea, Romania, in January 2006 in order to set up our counselling business. Over the first few months it gradually became clear that we couldn't be as effective as we wanted to because of both cultural and language barriers.

At around this time we started to realise that there was a huge need for training in therapy with children. As Romania was imminently preparing for membership of the European Union, the government made the major decision that a psychologist must be involved in every school, preschool and charity working with children.

While it was a clever decision politically to impress the European Union, it had been poorly thought through. Psychologists kept telling us that the degree course they had attended was entirely theoretical. There was no practical element or skills application at all. One man wrote to us slightly tongue-in-cheek: 'As a psychologist I'm expected to work with children. Tell me what children are and how I can work with them!'

At this point we thought again about our dream from several years back and how we could raise up specialists in working with children. As a result we began to develop about 25 one-day workshops in creative skills with children. They included sandtray, music, art, movement and puppets.

For the next three and a half years we travelled throughout Romania providing training in therapy with children using these courses. The participants were mainly psychologists, though other participants included child psychiatrists, social workers, counsellors and general practitioners. By the time we returned to the UK we had provided training for about 1000 professionals.

On our return we continued to offer the same one- and two-day courses we had prepared in Romania. But the dream of training counsellors actually to begin working with children and young people lived on. We started putting together four units of two days each, based on the material we used in Romania, that we could roll out as a full training course.

Around this time we had the opportunity and privilege to offer the first unit of two days at a national counselling conference in Derbyshire. The Association of Christian Counsellors (ACC) provided us with a large room to work with 24 counsellors.

After that, organisations of various types around Great Britain invited us to run the full four units for their counselling staff, supplemented by outside counsellors.

At this stage we wanted to be able to offer some sort of recognition to those who completed the course, assignments and written work. After a lot of paperwork on our part ACC gave our course Approved status. We could offer trainees who completed the course the Postgraduate Certificate in Therapy with Children and Families. Our dream at last was being fulfilled.

Before we retired in April 2014 we passed on our training skills to a number of highly qualified professionals so that they could run the course after we had stopped working.

Now the same material used in the course has been expanded into this book. While reading a book can never take the place of a training course, it can point the way, helping qualified counsellors make the transition from working only with adults to begin working with children and young people as well.

Our dream of 25 years ago is at last being fulfilled. Counsellors are seeing the huge potential of working therapeutically with clients under the age of 16.

Our dream at last has become a reality.

Roger & Christine Day
July 2018

Introduction

Welcome to an exciting new book that can help qualified counsellors and therapists to transfer their skills in working with adults to therapy with children age 3 to 11, young people and families.

This book is adapted from an eight-day training course that we developed several years ago and ran up and down the country before we retired in 2014. Other training events based on the same material have been run since then by trainers that we trained and approved.

The chapters in this book alternate between the *techniques* needed in working with children and young people and the *essentials* for practicing competently. In the techniques chapters there are dozens of activities and games that help children and young people to explore their emotions and make psychological changes using play. In fact, play has often been described as the child's 'work'. By contrast, the essentials chapters may seem uninteresting. Yet theoretical understanding and competence in practice are both vital if the counsellor is to make an ethical and responsible transition.

Two of the essentials chapters, *Trusting the Process* (chapter 1) and *Transferring Skills* (chapter 9), provide the key to making the transition from counselling adults using mainly talking skills to counselling children using mainly play. As such they are two of the most important chapters in the book.

At an early stage, even before working with children and young people, it is vital to have on board a supervisor who understands therapeutic work with clients under the age of 16. If the current supervisor isn't competent or interested in therapy with children and young people, a second supervisor with the specialised experience can be used. It is useful to have one or several sessions with this specialist supervisor before starting to see young clients.

In addition to a supervisor specialising in children and families it is very useful to have someone, such as a counselling colleague, that the therapist can ring if they become stuck. That way they can get immediate ideas and support before the next scheduled supervision session.

It is also useful – sometimes essential – to have personal therapy when working with children or young people. This client group can be hard work emotionally and can bring out deep issues in the counsellor that are best dealt with in the privacy of the counselling room. A counsellor having their own counsellor can also help them to become better at their work with young clients.

Reading about therapy with children, young people and families is one thing. Without face-to-face training and hands-on experience, however, the counsellor will almost certainly be ill-equipped to work therapeutically with people under the age of 16. Our strong advice, based on many years of experience, is that counsellors spend a minimum of eight days (or 48 hours) preparing themselves for this challenging yet rewarding task.

Our eight-day training course was designed to offer 20 per cent theory to 80 per cent practical. This seems a good balance of training for competent practice.

Theory can be gained through reading the chapters in this book interleaved with the practical ones, studying the recommended books and attending training events that focus on working with children and young people or creative approaches.

Practical skills can only be understood fully by the counsellor actually engaging in them. For instance, how could counsellors possibly understand what sandtray is like for a client without trying it for themselves? While it is possible to do a sandtray totally alone, it is best to have someone observing who can discuss and give feedback afterwards.

Ideas for engaging in practical skills with someone present include doing the activity in front of a supervisor or with a group of counsellor peers. It is amazing how powerful many of the activities are when the counsellor engages in them. If issues come up that the counsellor seems to find overwhelming, then it is perfectly appropriate (and highly recommended) to discuss concerns with their specialist supervisor before working with children and young people or at as early stage as possible after starting.

The recommended child observation and written report (chapter 7) could be submitted for discussion with the specialist supervisor.

When a child, young person or family is referred for therapy the counsellor will probably receive a certain amount of information. It's important for the counsellor to have a plan in their mind for the first session in case the client is stuck. Once they get to know the child or young person they will have a clearer picture of how to work. With this in mind, here are five scenarios for children/young people being referred for counselling. The person wanting to work with clients under 16 could work on their own or discuss each scenario with their peers or a supervisor. Then they can plan the first session using creative techniques based on the information they have here:

Jacob aged seven comes for therapy. Dad has just left the family. The child is refusing to go to school and won't let Mum out of his sight. How can you help?

Ten-year-old Hannah is being bullied at school. She is shy and withdrawn. Hannah doesn't seem to have many social skills. What strategies can you put in place to help her?

Six-year-old Toby is so shy that it is difficult to get a single words out of him. His parents have recently split up. How can you find out what he wants and needs when he won't talk to you?

Noah aged nine is being sent along by his mum, who says he is depressed. The family has also just moved to a new town and have no support system. Where do you start with Noah?

Leah is 13 and doesn't get on with her step-mum. As a result there is a lot of conflict in the family. Leah is willing to come for therapy. What creative ways could you use to help her?

Learning to work therapeutically with children and young people can be rewarding and even fun. The therapist will be far better equipped to engage with the child/young person when deep issues such as trauma and abuse come to the surface.

In a society that is becoming increasingly secular, many children have a spiritual dimension that counsellors are advised to take into account. Counsellors may well observe this when young children talk, for instance, about praying, God or angels.

How does the counsellor new to working with children and young people handle this dimension? In this book we have recommended objects in the therapy room to represent the spiritual. These could include a couple of tiny crosses, a holding cross, tiny religious pictures (icons), angels, beautiful little stones and gems, and a star or two. Using these symbols, some children may want to explore their own spiritual dimension. It is important to recognise, though, that some children may want to explore this dimension without such symbols.

The therapy room isn't the place for the therapist to tell child clients about their own belief system unless a client specifically asks. However, the counsellor's beliefs are important in the therapy room and can be used to good effect. We are both committed Christians and we would pray silently for child clients before and sometimes after a session. Occasionally we used an appropriate phrase from the Bible in a session.

One final recommendation is to read, reread and read again the book *Dibs: In search of self* (Axline, 1964/1990). This classic book tells the true story of a young boy called Dibs who came into therapy with huge problems and who worked through them using toys and play in a counselling setting. The book is both heart-rending and positive, and will give any counsellor hope for difficult clients of any age.

In that positive vein, we finish this Introduction with an article about working with children that we wrote many years ago:

What about the children?

He was small for his 11 years, with a bright smile to match his cheeky, dimpled face. Yet his eyes betrayed the inner hurt that counsellors learn to recognise. Soon he was sobbing harder than his presenting problem could ever have warranted.

'What is it that's really bothering you?' the counsellor asked.

'It's me best friend,' the lad replied. 'Two years ago he died of a brain tumour – and I think I murdered him.'

The sobbing increased to full-scale crying.

'What makes you think you murdered him?'

'Well – er – a week before he died I was play fighting with him and, see, he banged his head. That's why he got the brain tumour.'

How sad that this boy had suffered all those months of unbelievable agony because no one had explained to him that brain tumours aren't caused by a bump on the head! Not only that, but he hadn't been allowed to attend his best friend's funeral, and now no one he knew wanted to talk about the deceased boy.

The counsellor was able to help him sort out fact from fantasy and realise the importance of expressing his feelings and going through the grieving process.

Why is it that children are the last to be helped?

■ *'We didn't want them hurt any more than they were so we kept them away from the funeral.'*
■ *'We didn't discuss our separation because the kids were already fed up with our constant arguing.'*
■ *'After having to testify against the abuser we just wanted her to get on with life and forget about it.'*

Adults seek counselling to resolve issues in their own lives. But what about the children? They have feelings, too. Just because they're small it doesn't mean they don't know what's going on. And anyway, at least 90 per cent of issues brought up in counselling have their origins firmly rooted in the first 10 years of life.

Why do people have to wait until they are in their 30s or even 60s to deal with problems that could have been tackled so much easier when they were four or 14 – and therefore much nearer to source?

And why are so few trained counsellors willing to help the under-16s? It's almost as if they are scared of little clients, worried that their carefully-developed skills with adults will be ineffective or even damaging when adapted to children's needs.

It's a fact that children aren't a soft touch. They might be vulnerable, as in the case of those who are sexually abused by an adult, but they're certainly not easily manipulated. No amount of persuasion by the counsellor, for instance, will get them to say what they don't want to say.

In our experience, providing there is a firm contract in place, there is little or no danger of a child's psyche being destroyed at the hands of a caring counsellor.

Of course, counselling children and families requires specialised training and experience. One important difference is in the way children are referred for counselling.

Jean Campion writes: 'Unlike adults who from time to time complain about, and seek help to change, certain things in their lives, children tend to take their personal circumstances for granted, and even to blame themselves when they find themselves in disagreeable situations which are not their fault, showing their distress and confusion indirectly through their behaviour. Thus, a child is much more likely to reach a counsellor because someone is worried by his unusual, troubled or troublesome behaviour than because he has asked for help' (Campion, 1991).

There are wide open gaps in helping children. Much energy by statutory and voluntary groups is quite rightly put into protecting children from abuse, for instance. But relatively little in-depth counselling is provided to help heal the deep emotional scars that will otherwise be with the person for the rest of their life.

Similarly, almost no counselling is offered to children who sexually abuse other children. This growing phenomenon is, in our experience as former private practitioners, under-reported because parents fear the break-up of the family if they talk to social services. A helpful book on this almost taboo subject is **Children and Young People as Abusers: An agenda for action (**Bentovim, et al, 1991).

Like adults, children need the three Ps (Crossman, 1966; Steiner, 1968) in the counselling relationship:

Potency: 'I'm strong enough to listen to the worst possible things you've done or that have been done to you.' 'I can cope when you feel like shouting at me because I remind you of a member of your family.'

Protection: 'I'm on your side.' 'You won't be abandoned.'

Permission: 'You don't need to hide your tears when you're here.' 'I'll let you express your rage without hurting yourself or me.'

In our counselling work with children we learnt to adapt adult concepts to our young clients' needs. This was helped especially by our therapeutic model based on Transactional Analysis (TA).

Unlike psychoanalysis, TA uses everyday words, such as describing the three ego states in terms of Parent, Adult and Child.

Even a preschool child can understand the three basics of TA:

'People are OK.
Everyone has the capacity to think.
People decide their own destiny, and these decisions can be changed' (Stewart & Joines, 1987, page 6).

When we worked with very young children, we were both usually in the counselling room. This provided a safeguard and a balanced approach. We invited parents of younger children to stay in on the sessions, with the child's clear permission. Often parents who choose to stay found that they became just as involved in the healing process as the child.

Using Egan's three-stage model (Egan, 1975/2013), we carefully adapted TA to the needs of each individual child client:

Stage 1 – Exploration

We emphasised relationship building, entering the child's world in terms of understanding likes and dislikes, fun and fears, fantasies and frights. It might have involved drawing together, working together in the sandtray, playing a silly game or even running around!

We tended to work carefully on the client's self-image, helping them to overcome such faulty thinking as 'I'm no good', 'I'm useless', 'Everyone's better than me', 'No one loves me', 'I'm not special', 'I hate myself'. We built up the client's self-image with positive unconditional strokes (Stewart & Joines, 1987, pages 73-81). They included phrases such as: 'You're special', 'I like you', 'You're lovable'.

Children would come back excitedly telling us, 'I gave a positive stroke to my mum, and she gave me one back!' They were absolutely delighted to realise that by giving a positive stroke at home or school they often received one back.

Another important element is to help the client get their Adult thinking into control ('in the driving seat'). This is done by strengthening the client's Adult, by decontaminating Parent prejudices and deconfusing Child fantasies. We would perhaps bring a client out of a traumatic experience by addressing them in their Adult: 'Sit up straight. Tell me your full name. How old are you? What's three add six? . . .'

Feelings are often repressed in a hurting child, and we helped clients express them – squeezing a stress ball, tearing paper or punching pillows. We used specialised therapeutic games such as **All About Me** (Barnardo's) and **Angry Monster Machine** (Childswork).

In this exploratory stage we helped identify feelings expressed nonverbally: thumb-sucking, curling into a foetal position, 'itchy' eyes (suppressing tears), restlessness and bed-wetting.

When one seven-year-old boy started thumb-sucking in the counselling room Christine pointed it out gently. This raised the mother's hackles. 'If you suck your thumb you'll get threadworms again,' she said, reinforcing a Parent message the boy had heard many times. Gradually we worked with the client and the mother on this issue until he was now happy to suck his thumb when he was sad, even while cuddling up to his mother.

Stage 2 – New Understanding

Two- or three-chair work is a Gestalt/TA technique we found useful at this stage. This involved getting the young client to imagine a relative sitting on an empty chair in front of them and speaking to that imaginary person.

One 12-year-old girl confronted her step-dad in the empty chair in front of her, became angry and then exclaimed afterwards, 'I feel as though a weight has been lifted off me!' Eventually, the girl was better able to contact her feelings about the step-dad, and the man came back to live at home.

An adolescent boy's mixed-up (contaminated) beliefs about himself had been based on a couple of teachers telling him at a young age that he was 'unteachable'. We used two-chair work with him to decontaminate the beliefs he had developed as a result of those teachers' unthinking and cruel remarks.

A clear understanding of symbiosis had come in useful on several occasions. We explained to clients the symbiotic relationship of a young child and his mother and the importance of gradually breaking away in early childhood. If this is not done, there is a tendency to assume that others know their unspoken needs (unhealthy symbiosis).

Goal-setting is an important part of this stage of the process. We often gave child clients fun homework to do between sessions – making a Feelings Book, designing a poster of things the child was good at. It was also a useful way of getting a family to interact.

Stage 3 – Action
In terms of relearning, we used an adapted form of Gestalt/drama therapy to help clients understand their decision better. One 10-year-old client had developed a good relationship with the lodger, a man in his 30s. The lodger was now leaving the house and getting married.

Our client saw this as a form of betrayal. Jealousy and anger were characteristic of his feelings. This was combined with an admission on his part of sexual attraction to the lady concerned!

After several sessions of working through these issues, we got the client to sit between the engaged man and woman, all three hugging each other. We then got the client to sit facing the couple and say, 'I let you go,' symbolically severing the previous relationship.

Eric Berne describes the ideal end-product for counselling as: autonomy, 'manifested by the release or recovery of three capacities: awareness, spontaneity and intimacy' (Berne, 1964. See pages 158-160.) Our goal in working with child clients was to help them know who they were and what they were capable of, to be free beings and to enjoy closeness in their family and in other healthy relationships.

1
Trusting the process

Most counselling courses specifically exclude skills in working with clients under the age of 16. As a result, many trainees qualify as counsellors with the belief that they would have to start again if they wanted to counsel children and young people. This book is intended to show that this isn't necessarily the case.

Counsellors working with adults already have many of the needed qualities and skills for working with children and young people. This chapter, along with chapter 9 called *Transferring skills,* aims to show the main differences between the two and how the counsellor can start to transfer their skills.

Working with over 16s usually involves what is known as *talking therapy;* working with children of most ages involves predominantly *play.* This fits with the phrase: 'Play is the child's work.' Children play to understand and act out what they observe and experience around them. It makes sense, therefore, to use play in a therapeutic context to help them solve their emotional difficulties.

With talking therapy the counsellor can usually see what changes the client is making. With play this isn't so easy. Can play in therapy really result in the same kind of changes that talking therapy can achieve? It is important for the therapist working with children to accept that such changes really *can* happen.

An important phrase in understanding what is happening in therapy with children is:

Trust the process.

Some therapists may find trusting the process difficult to accept at first, yet numerous counsellors working with children will acknowledge the truth behind it. Children will often change in therapy even if the counsellor doesn't recognise the change that is happening.

This leads to the importance of the developing counsellor with children and young people starting to use their *intuition.* This can help in understanding what is happening in the child and what is needed to help the child with further therapeutic change. Such intuition in the therapy room may take some time to develop. A useful popular book that provides a good introduction to intuition and is well worth reading is *Blink,* by Malcolm Gladwell (Gladwell, 2005).

Measured outcomes

Many counsellors starting to work with children and young people will become part of an organisation such as a school or counselling centre. These often require or certainly value measured outcomes in therapy (often referred to as *clinical governance).* Even independent counsellors will find it helpful to measure how well the work is doing with their young clients.

A useful measure can be provided by using Robert Goodman's SDQs (Strengths and Difficulties Questionnaires – see Goodman, 1997). This outcome-based approach fits in well with statutory and government agencies as well as schools, which are interested in positive, quantifiable results for children rather than the child merely 'feeling better'. SDQs compare the child's emotional state before and after therapy. They are questionnaires that are given to parents, carers, social workers and teachers before, at halfway stage and after the therapy. Older children also fill them in. In 70 per cent of cases the SDQs show improvement in children's coping mechanisms as a result of therapy.

Details about how to use SDQs are beyond the scope of this book. If more information is needed there is a helpful website containing plenty of information about using them.

The actual forms in various languages can be downloaded from this site free of charge:

www.sdqinfo.com

Quadrant of understanding

An effective way of understanding the process of therapy with children and young people involves a quadrant model taken from play therapy. In this book we have deliberately avoided using the term *play therapist* because a counsellor would need a lot more training before they could use it to describe themselves. But play therapy has a lot to teach the counsellor as they develop skills in working with clients under 16.

The *Play Therapy Dimensions Model* (see page 32) is based on a book of the same name (Yasenik & Gardner, 2004/2012) that comes from the well-respected Rocky Mountain Play Therapy Institute in Calgary, Alberta, Canada. This model explores how a counsellor can assess and enhance their practice as a therapist working with children. It helps to track the counsellor's own process and that of their client so that the counsellor is providing the best possible approach for each child they work with. This model is especially useful in supervision to reflect on work already done and consider effective ways forward.

We will only give a brief outline here. The counsellor and supervisor may want to read more on the internet or get the book if they want to explore further this model and its uses.

Much of the book you are reading focuses on activities initiated by the counsellor. This is known as *directive therapy.* When the child is left to take the initiative in aspects of their therapy this is called *nondirective therapy.* This is the therapeutic approach in *Dibs: In search of self* (Axline, 1964/1990), a book we have already recommended all therapists to read. The Play Therapy Dimensions Model incorporates both nondirective and directive therapy. It also covers what is clearly understood in the therapy (conscious) and distinguishes it from what is not at all understood (unconscious).

The model consists of two lines that intersect to form four quadrants.

The *Directiveness* line is horizontal. At the extreme left, the therapy is becoming completely nondirective. This is the way many play therapists are trained, with the belief that the child knows how to solve their problems in their own way. At the extreme right the counsellor is giving clear instructions to the child and they are responding. Even the most extreme child-centred therapist will become directive to some extent, such as choosing toys that meet the client's needs.

Then there is the *Consciousness* line, which is vertical. At the very top the child is working in a highly conscious, cognitive way. At the very bottom they are working at an unconscious level. The reason for working at this unconscious level is that children often need to have emotional distance when dealing with painful issues. The child therefore engages in symbolic play using the play objects.

These two lines create the four quadrants of the dimensions model:

Nonintrusive responding

On the bottom left there is a section known as *nonintrusive responding*. This is not the same as nondirective. Here the therapist joins in the play only when the child invites them to do so. Comments are reflective, tracking the child's play. For instance, the therapist might say: 'That tiger sounds angry,' or 'It seems you're still not sure about this play room.' A child who has difficulty structuring play may need to move to one of the other quadrants.

Cofacilitation

In the bottom right there is *cofacilitation*. In this quadrant therapeutic activities, including interpretations, stay within the play. The therapist develops what Jungian therapists might term 'soft hypotheses', and these are tested out through the play or by putting specific toys out in advance. The therapist becomes more immersed than in the previous quadrant. The therapist uses their intuition to cofacilitate the play and move it forward to dealing with the client's presenting issues. For instance, with a boy who is being bullied the therapist might introduce into the joint play: 'They're after us. They keep attacking us. There's only a few of us and so many of them!'

Active utilisation

In the top left there is *active utilisation.* In this quadrant, the child initiates the play and the therapist occasionally gives interpretive comments that trigger conscious responses from the child. Key elements of the play are interpreted and these can be used as a way of resolving problems. For instance, a child who has seen domestic violence at home may cover their ears when a play character makes a loud noise. The therapist in this quadrant may then say: 'That loud noise may seem scary because of what happened at home.'

Open discussion and exploration

In the top right quadrant there is *open discussion and exploration.* In this quadrant the therapist chooses play activities that may help the child gradually to process their difficulties. This is often the quadrant used when running therapy groups. It is useful when working with a child using a brief model of, say, only four or six sessions. It is also helpful when the child feels 'stuck' or doesn't want to go too deep into unconscious stuff. The therapist could then suggest a 'light' activity such as a therapeutic board game or a drawing exercise.

The dimensions model can help clarify where the counsellor is in the healing process with a child or young person. By observing the child's responses, verbally and through body language, they can vary the quadrant they are working from. They can also adjust their level of involvement in the therapy.

Play therapy dimensions diagram

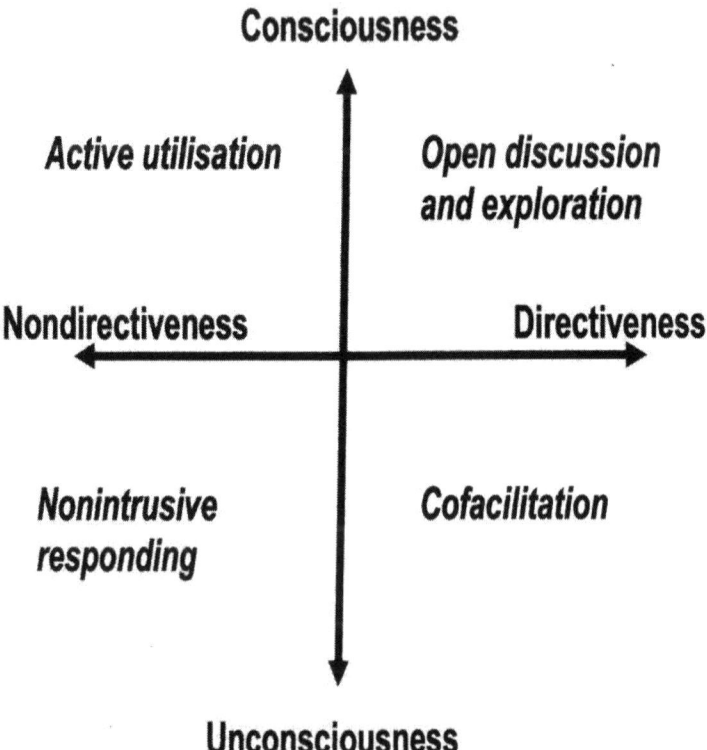

Consciousness

Active utilisation

Open discussion and exploration

Nondirectiveness

Directiveness

Nonintrusive responding

Cofacilitation

Unconsciousness

adapted from Play Therapy Dimensions Model: A decision-making guide for integrative play therapists, by Lorri Yasenik & Ken Gardner. London: Jessica Kingsley Publishers, 2012.

2
Art in therapy

One of the most natural things for a child to do is to draw, paint or create something in clay or junk materials (sometimes known as 3D materials). Give a child some paper and pens and suggest they draw and the response is usually instant. The same applies to other art materials. For children and young people who are encouraged to be creative, it is an enjoyable activity. Painting and other art expressions are pleasant, sometimes even exciting.

Although the counsellor is probably not a qualified art therapist, art activities such as painting, drawing and 3D modelling in a therapeutic context provide ways for the child or young person to express their feelings, explain trauma and deal with problems.

They are also useful for the therapist. For instance, Cathy Malchiodi (2001) writes: 'A drawing can provide information on developmental, emotional and cognitive functioning, hasten expression of hidden traumas, and convey ambiguous or contradictory feelings and perceptions.'

Children's pictures and creations usually have meaning. The trouble is that what means one thing to a child means something completely different to another child. For instance, an egg-box crocodile with its mouth open could mean aggression and anger. But it could also mean the child's need for nourishment. A painting of a mountain might be something that the child is conquering or it could be an obstacle in the way.

So how does the therapist know what a particular drawing or piece of art means? The first thing is to ask the child or young person. Instead of asking the child Roger once said something like: 'That's an interesting fire engine.' The child replied: 'No, it's a bus!' The therapeutic edge on that session had been lost. From then on we learned to ask the child rather than assuming we knew what message was being put across.

Often as the child talks about the art, they make changes to it that later are seen as part of the therapeutic changes that are happening internally. In the same way, in transactional analysis we believe that everyone early on in life makes decisions that lead to their script and that they can change those decisions, such as through therapy, leading to 'cure' (see Stewart & Joines, 1987, pages 268-270).

It is best not to comment on the piece of art until the therapist knows what is being conveyed. In life outside the therapy room it is helpful to say positive things to children about their worth and about what they create. But when artwork is being used by children in creative therapy it is useful, at least to start with, to be neutral. If the child has enjoyed drawing and this is obvious, this can be reflected back to the child: 'It seemed like you really enjoyed doing that drawing,' etc. Later on positive comments can be added once the therapist is clear about the direction the therapy is going.

Drawing

Introduction

Drawing is a vital tool in assessing and working with young clients. 'The popularity of drawing techniques in the assessment of children can be attributed to two factors,' write Frick, Barry & Kamphaus (1996, page 245). 'First, unlike other projective techniques that require substantial verbal ability often exceeding the verbal capacity of very young children, drawing techniques are primarily nonverbal. Second, most children are familiar and comfortable with drawing, so it is an enjoyable assessment context for a child.'

Post-Yungian psychotherapist John Daly (2005) points out that there are three basic types of drawing:

- *Series drawings*
- *Spontaneous drawings*
- *Requested drawings*

Series

When a child paints a series of drawings they are often highly symbolic. Hopefully over several weeks the series will evolve and change as the child gains emotional understanding. Questions to ask the child who uses series drawings:

Tell me what's in the picture?
What went on in the story before the picture?
What happens next?

Spontaneous

Repetition of spontaneous pictures may be an indication that the child is stuck in therapy. This is particularly the case where the child has obsessive compulsive tendencies. In other cases a child may draw the same thing over and over again without ever explaining what they are doing. They are resolving their problems themselves, with the therapist witnessing the process. For them it is easier to draw it than to say it.

Requested

The therapist might want to request the child or young person to draw something on a particular theme. This can be done through giving the child a preprinted photocopy and asking them to do a drawing within it. The excellent book *Draw on Your Emotions* (Sunderland, 1997), although expensive, contains a wealth of preprinted pages that can be photocopied free of copyright. Many of them are ideal for therapy with children.

Another way is to ask the child to draw a specific theme. Examples include:

- *A visit to the doctor.*
- *My family.*
- *The happiest time of my life.*

Requested drawings can be used effectively across cultural and language barriers.

The therapist was working with a group of looked-after children in a remote rural area of Eastern Europe. Through the translator he asked the children to find a space in the room separate from the others and draw something that was important to them.

At the end of the session they each handed in their drawing. Two sisters had drawn pictures of trees that looked similar, even though they had worked in separate parts of the room. The younger one had produced two drawings, one of a tree with smiling faces all over it, the other solid black and featureless. This second picture she kept hidden behind her back until the very last moment.

Later the story of the two sisters emerged. Although true it sounded like something out of one of Grimm's Fairy Tales. The girls' mother died and their father handed them over to their grandmother. She was unwilling to raise them so one night she led them into the forest and tied them to a tree, leaving them there for dead. Early the next morning they were found by a woodcutter who released them and contacted the local police.

The drawings were the girls' first steps to exploring and resolving the grief and major post-traumatic stress that affected them so deeply. While they were unable or unwilling to talk about their experiences, drawing provided just what they needed at that time.

Child development in drawing

Studying a child's initial drawings in therapy can be a useful guide to the kind of difficulties they might have. In order to do that it is important to have some idea of what may be considered 'normal' development as seen in children's drawings. For more on drawings and child development see Rhoda Kellogg's book *Analysing Children's Drawings* (1970) or Bob Steele's book *Draw Me a Story* (1997).

Scribbling stage – age 18 months upwards
At this stage drawings are meaningful and often full of joy just for the pleasure of drawing. Children hold pencils and explore the art materials in a playful way. When asked they will often point out what they have drawn.

Scribbling tends to change from uncontrolled to controlled movements of the pencil. Examples include forming a circle, vertical and horizontal lines and creating the self-portrait. Gradually the child's drawings become more boundaried.

Pre-schematic stage – age two to four
Here drawings become more complex. Favourite colours are often used rather than the 'correct' colours. Drawings of people are simple, often 'tadpole' drawings – the person has a very large head and tiny body with lines to represent arms and legs. Ask the child to put a tummy button on the person and they seem to know exactly where it should go, even if it is below the actual drawing!

Often animals show three dimensions in one plane, objects appear to float in space, and interiors and exteriors are shown at the same time.

Towards the end of this stage a very important psychological stage is reached in which a drawing of a house often equates to the self.

Schematic stage – age five to eight
At this stage drawings start to become in proportion and detailed. Colours are more realistic and often stereotypical (grass is green, sky is blue). Objects within one picture will be repeated in several other pictures. A baseline and a skyline will start to form. Pictures become much more expressive, often accompanied by verbal stories about each picture.

By age eight clothes start to appear on human figures. Sometimes dots are used to show movement or direction of, say, a football, or someone diving into the water.

A picture of a house usually includes a chimney with smoke (often at right angles to the roof), fruit on a tree and the sun in the sky.

Pre-teen stage – age nine to 11

At this stage drawings have become more detailed and complex. Spatial awareness has usually developed considerably. Before this stage children often put all the perspectives in one flat drawing. By age 12 they generally show only three sides to, say, a cube.

This is the stage when children may become frustrated about not drawing accurately and express phrases such as: 'I can't draw.' This is often not helped by significant adults making negative comments about their drawing ability.

Cultural differences

Drawings reflect the culture the child is from. The typical western child will draw a 'cottage loaf' person with an oval body, round hands and feet, and arms and legs with parallel lines.

On the other hand, a child from Nigeria might produce the 'square person' with a square or rectangular body. Children from south-west Africa may typically produce the 'triangle person', consisting of a body with triangles pointing towards each other in the middle of the body.

Even more unusual, a child from an Indian village may put parts of the body along a vertical line, with the head at the top.

Learning difficulties

A child with learning difficulties will usually show in their drawings approximately their developmental age rather than their actual age. Sometimes, though, the drawings may seem even younger than this because of emotional trauma or bullying.

House-tree-person

An approach particularly useful in working with children and young people is the House-tree-person drawing. This was developed by John Buck in the 1940s as a way of exploring an individual's personality characteristics.

Psychologist Dr Richard Niolon writes: 'The basic assumption is that we project things on to drawings that tell us about us. Houses reflect our ideas about family, trees are part of us we have difficulty facing (since it is easy to project things on to a tree since it isn't like us) and people are parts of us we mostly feel OK to acknowledge. Some of the interpretations you make are symbolic and require knowing a bit about the drawing. So you have to ask questions' (Niolon, 2003).

In working therapeutically with children, the therapist simply asks them to draw the three items on one piece of paper, repeating the request until the child has finished. Then ask open-ended questions. Analysis or interpretation are best saved for individual reflection or for supervision at a later stage.

Questions start with statements: 'Tell me about the house' etc.

Look for a *house* with windows and accessible door with a handle. The handle will vary according to the child's culture. For instance, children from the UK will generally draw a round handle, while people in parts of Eastern Europe will tend to draw a single line at right angles to represent a door handle. Most children of any culture, even ones where chimneys are rare, will put a chimney on the house with smoke coming out of it – a good indication that there is life in the house. If there isn't a chimney with smoke or windows, state something like: 'The chimney doesn't have any smoke' or 'The windows seem small', then wait for the child's response.

Supplementary questions about the drawn house could include:

- *Who lives here?*
- *What happens inside?*
- *What's it like living there?*

The therapist may look for evidence of roots in the *tree* as well as leaves and fruit on the branches. If there isn't any fruit they can point this out to the child.

They can ask follow-up questions:

- *What kind of tree is it?*
- *Has anyone tried to cut it down?*
- *Who takes care of the tree?*

The *person* that has been drawn ideally is well-defined and proportional to the rest of the drawing. If the person is too big the therapist simply asks: 'How does the person get into the house?'

Supplementary questions could include:

- *What does the person like to do?*
- *How old are they?*
- *What's it like being that person?*

The three drawn objects will generally be on a real or imagined baseline on the page. Sometimes there is no baseline and the drawings start from the very bottom of the piece of paper. In our experience this indicates a very small child with little history or someone with abandonment issues whose history is unclear or unknown.

The result of exploring these three drawings can be revealing for the child and can give the therapist a basic understanding of some of the issues the child may need to deal with in therapy.

Therapeutic purpose: Drawing is very useful to help the counsellor assess the young client's emotional needs. We have also used it as a form of clinical governance, with one drawing done before therapy and one towards the end. Then the two drawings are compared to see what internal changes have happened within the child or young person.

Cartoon magic

The book *Cartoon Magic* (Mills & Crowley, 1989) is about children using cartoon characters that can come alongside the child in their imagination to help the child at times of need. This technique involves three steps:

■ *First, get the child to draw a picture on a piece of paper of what their worry, fear or pain looks like.*
■ *Second, on a separate piece of paper draw a picture of the cartoon helper such as a superhero that they know could help with their problem.*
■ *Third, on another piece of paper, draw how the problem would look when it is all better, with the helper/superhero now with the child.*

The *all better* pictures represent the children's own unconscious healing process. They remind children that 'all better' really *does* exist somewhere within themselves.

Parents can also be encouraged to leave pencil and paper by the bedside for the child to draw an 'all better' picture using their favourite cartoon character if they suffer from recurring nightmares.

Therapeutic purpose: Developing a personal support system for young children, especially in dealing with fear, helping young clients to discover their own resilience.

Squiggle drawing

Psychiatrist Donald Winnicott (1971) invented an exercise called the Squiggle Drawing where client and therapist create a drawing together by taking it in turns using the same piece of paper. The idea was that it was a form of building the therapeutic relationship.

We have found it useful in our work with children and young people, though it has its limitations. For instance, Dr

Jean Thurow, who wrote extensively on her work using the squiggle game, wondered if Winnicott needed a 'sixth sense' to respond effectively to a child. She writes: 'I often did not understand their meanings and found the communicative process hard to follow. I occasionally found myself disturbed by my own images drawn during the game. I could not tell if my drawings were a further expression of the child's difficulties or if they came from my own inner world. I could not always tell if my images were useful or harmful' (Thurow, 1989).

Despite these limitations, it may be useful to use it with a child to break the ice and see what emerges. It's a case of simply take it in turns to make a squiggle pattern on the paper using the same pen and continue each other's drawing.

As with many of the other activities in this book, it could prove useful to do a squiggle drawing with a colleague who understands psychological processes before attempting it with a child.

Therapeutic purpose: Building the therapeutic alliance, empowering the young person, the joy of creating something together.

Painting

Permission to paint in therapy is a valuable treasure to most child and adolescent clients. It might result in mess but the experience is therapeutic in itself. And a young person's paintings can reveal much about what is going on in their mind.

Donald Winnicott writes: 'It is only in being creative that the individual discovers the self' (Winnicott, 1971, page 54).

Others also have their thoughts. American artist Georgia O'Keeffe says: 'I found I could say things with colour and shape that I couldn't say any other way – things I had no words for.'

'Art is a place for children to learn to trust their ideas themselves, and to explore what is possible,' writes child art expert MaryAnn Kohl. 'Art is as natural as sunshine and as vital as nourishment.'

Simply pointing out to a child or young person where the brushes, paints and paper are kept may be all that is needed for them to start exploring their emotional issues through paint. Below are three ideas for a more directive approach:

■ *I invite you to use colour to paint a picture on paper of who you are. Try doing it with the hand you don't use for writing.*
■ *Use the paints to do a picture without using brushes. It's OK here to get your fingers and hands covered in paint. When you've finished tell the story that you've painted.*
■ *I'll put on some music and, when it starts, paint with the rhythm of the music.*

Therapeutic purpose: Creativity, fun, self-discovery, enabling the counsellor to begin understanding the client's internal processes.

Craft/3D materials

Children also love to use 3D materials such as modelling clay and 'glorious junk', as it has been called.

Modelling can be done with natural clay, clays that dry hard without the need to fire them, modelling materials that can be reused, and home-made or shop-bought playdough. Choose what kind fits best with the therapy room environment and the clients.

Lynne Souter-Anderson (2015) writes: 'Searching to understand and make meaning of difficult and traumatic situations and confusing experiences is possible when children and adolescents work with clay, for the relevance of the process is something immediately grasped and understood by the young. Working in clay thus can be considered a "universal language", crossing language and cultural barriers' (page xviii).

Young clients can be shown the clay and left to engage in nondirective therapy for themselves. Guided clay therapy ideas include:

■ *Create your family in the clay and then talk about each person.*
■ *Show your dream in the clay.*
■ *Make something in clay that might possibly **stop** you feeling better. (When it is finished ask: What do you want to do with it now? The range of ideas for disposing of it can be wide.)*

Much of what is put in recycling bins can be used instead for junk modelling. Then it can be returned to recycling after the therapy is completely finished.

Cathy James (2015) says: 'Junk modelling is creative, free, environmentally friendly and brain boosting.'

As with clay, child clients can simply be turned loose with the 'glorious junk', or they can be given directive suggestions:

■ *Make a junk model that could support you when things get difficult.*
■ *Create a safe place using the junk materials.*
■ *Use the materials to create something or someone that will protect you.*

Therapeutic purpose: Creative fun, building confidence and self-esteem; enabling the client to empower themselves when things become tough.

3
Safeguarding

For anyone planning to work therapeutically with children and young people it is important to have a policy in which the therapist commits to protecting and safeguarding child clients while they are in therapy. If the therapist is working for an organisation, the counsellor is well advised to ask to see their safeguarding policy. If they don't have one, or the therapist considers the policy inadequate, it is important to encourage the organisation to develop one or revise the one they already have. The same applies if the therapist is working in private practice.

The policy document *Working together to Safeguard Children,* published in March 2015 by the UK government, says:

'Whilst local authorities play a lead role, safeguarding children and protecting them from harm is everyone's responsibility. Everyone who comes into contact with children and families has a role to play . . . Local agencies, including the police and health services, also have a duty under section 11 of the Children Act 2004 to ensure that they consider the need to safeguard and promote the welfare of children when carrying out their functions. Under section 10 of the same Act, a similar range of agencies are required to cooperate with local authorities to promote the well-being of children in each local authority area . . . This cooperation should exist and be effective at all levels of the organisation, from strategic level through to operational delivery. Professionals working in agencies with these duties are responsible for ensuring that they fulfil their role and responsibilities in a manner consistent with the statutory duties of their employer' (HM Government, 2015, page 5).

Appendix A of this book contains a detailed outline safeguarding policy developed for counselling children. It is free of copyright. Therapists are invited to read it carefully and, if they want to, use it as a model for developing their own or their organisation's policies. Included in it are important issues about safety in the therapy room, boundaries, DBS checks and on-line safety.

Updating policies

Policies need regularly updating as changes in society take place. For instance, a safeguarding policy about working with children may now need to include rules about whether or not the counsellor makes contact with clients under the age of 16 using on-line messaging services. Could such contact be deemed as stalking? If so, how could this be prevented?

Similarly, does there need to be some sort of safeguard to prevent the counsellor having under-16s who aren't family members as friends on social media?

These and other aspects will need to be discussed and taken into account when updating policies.

Therapy room

Most counselling and therapy takes place in a room with the door shut. When working with children it is sometimes useful to leave the door slightly ajar, even if it compromises confidentiality. Examples could be the child with extreme anxiety or claustrophobia or the one who has been subjected to sexual abuse behind a closed door. Not only does the client feel safe but the therapist can feel less vulnerable. Using a room with glass in the door is another way to help a child feel safe.

Another example is sometimes allowing children to leave the therapy room. The normal rule is to stay in the room until the session finishes. Therapists could consider an exception for children who have experienced being locked in their bedroom as a punishment and those who have not been allowed out of a room until they have engaged in a sexual activity with an abuser. In these rare instances the child may be given permission to leave the room as often as they need to.

Safe touch

Children and young people who have emotional difficulties often need physical contact. With this in mind several years ago we developed a Safe Touch policy that we believe ensures children get what they need without compromising safeguarding. Our initial idea has been accepted and used by others in developing their own safeguarding policies. This aspect is included in the safeguarding policy in Appendix A.

There are five principles:

1. Always have other people in sight
The therapist avoids being on their own with a child of any age.

2. Ensure that the child wants the physical contact being offered
Where possible make eye contact with the child and indicate with gestures or verbally what is proposed, waiting for the child's clear agreement. If the therapist believes a child may have been abused, it is important to avoid physical contact until the child has learned the difference between 'good' touching and 'bad' touching. This may take many sessions to build up the trust needed.

3. Touch in appropriate areas only
Consciously avoid touching the child in areas of the body that would be covered by a swimming costume. Touching the child's leg above the knee is also generally not acceptable.

4. Be cautious about having a child on your lap

Men especially are strongly advised to avoid children sitting on their laps. In exceptional circumstances they may let a small child sit on the knee end of their lap.

5. Avoid face-to-face hugging of a girl who has begun to develop

This is especially important with men. Instead of a face-to-face hug, the counsellor could try an arm on the shoulder 'sideways hug'. This satisfies the older girl's need for closeness and avoids inappropriate physical contact.

Making contact

Once a child client is OK about touch, the therapist can introduce safe touch activities as needed. Here are some suggestions:

■ *Contact using High Five. Then try a lighthearted High Five: Give me five, on the side, up above, down below [move hand], too slow.*

■ *Various handshakes to make contact: normal handshake, then entwined fingers handshake. Lighthearted handshakes include: Train Driver [move both hands in a circle like a train wheel], Milkman [squeeze and release the other's hand as if milking a cow], Fish Salesman [brush hand flat across the other's palm as if handling a wet fish]. Road Worker [move both hands rapidly up and down as if using a pneumatic drill]. Devise together fancy handshakes.*

Sir Richard Bowlby, the son of the great attachment expert John Bowlby, has spoken about a 25-year experiment in which children (boys and girls) who are played with by their fathers in creative, meaningful and physically close ways at the age of two develop more emotionally healthy throughout their childhood. Right up to the age of 22 there is a significant difference between children whose fathers played with them as toddlers and those who didn't.

He says: 'Researchers have found that children who excel in social situations as young adults, had mothers who provided an enduring secure base and a positive model for intimate relationships within the family, and fathers who had provided exciting play and interactive challenges. There seem to be two separate attachment roles for two separate but equally significant functions – one attachment role is to provide love and security, and the other attachment role is to engage in exciting and challenging experiences' (Freeman, Newland & Coyl, 2010, page 26).

It is interesting that consistently about 70 per cent of child clients are boys. Without in any way taking the place of the important work of fathers and mothers in clients' lives, here are some ideas that most boys may enjoy:

- Demonstrate light friendly punch on the arm.
- Feel client's arm muscles.
- Massage shoulders.

4
Stories and visualisation

All children and young people – and almost all adults – love a good story. Stories can be used in therapy with children, young people and families in different ways. Clients can create their own story as part of understanding themselves. They can also listen to stories in a guided way through creative visualisation. Whatever way the story is used, it often has a powerful effect.

Stories

Families in many cultures – including Irish, Asian and Eastern European – have their own stories that are passed from one generation to another. If a therapist is working cross-culturally with clients from these groups it is important to use the stories that emerge in the therapy, which may well be linked with the family stories. From them clients can explore and start to understand their emotions.

Most other young clients from Western countries will have stories familiar to them that are outside of their cultural context. These also work well in therapy.

Children and young people love stories and, with the right support, have the ability to use stories to heal their own hurts. In all therapy with children and young people the therapist uses their intuition to hear the story the child is telling through play and other nonverbal ways. Then in various ways that same story can help the child to resolve their own problems.

One approach, probably beyond the scope of this book, is narrative play therapy, which has developed over the last 30 years. It was founded by Ann Cattanach, Sue Jennings and Brenda Meldrum. These were all dramatherapists and saw the importance of finding the story or narrative emerging from the child's play and using it in the therapeutic process.

Ann Cattanach writes about narrative play therapy: 'It is about people talking, empathic understanding, sharing creativity – not power and control centred on the therapist' (Cattanach, 1988/2002, page 7). For further information on this subject we highly recommend the book *Narrative Play Therapy: Theory and practice,* edited by Aideen Taylor de Faoite (2011).

My story

This is an activity that can be done with a group of children, a family or an individual young person. The therapist can join in if they would like to. They invite each person to talk about what their favourite story was when they were under the age of seven. If the client is seven or younger, there is no need to mention that age. If a person isn't sure which story is their favourite, they can be asked to mention just one of the stories they know. It might actually *be* their favourite, even if they can't identify it as such. Once they have said their stories, ask them to think about why they think it might be their favourite.

As with other therapeutic activities, it is vital that the therapist doesn't interpret the story for the client.

Therapeutic purpose: This activity can help to assess children's and young people's emotional needs both now and earlier in their lives. It can also trigger memories and emotions that can be explored in forthcoming sessions.

Stories in therapy

Stories have been used since the beginning of time to communicate concepts, explain ideas and understand the reactions of others. Jesus used stories about camels, sheep, trees and seeds to help the people of his time to understand his concepts.

The ancient Greeks told the story of **Tantalus,** who through eternity saw food and drink but couldn't eat or drink it. Psychotherapist Eric Berne used this story to help people understand why they can *Never* achieve. This was one of several script types he proposed, based on the Greek stories, including:

Arachne – *Always* has to spin webs.
Jason – *Until* he completed tasks he could not be king.
Damocles – *After* enjoying being a king the sword falls.
Sisyphus – *Almost* pushing the stone up, then it falls back.
Philemon and Baucis – *Open ended* because they were turned into laurel trees for good behaviour. (See Berne, 1972/1975, pages 236-237.)

Berne also took existing fairy stories such as Cinderella (op cit, pages 264-271) and Little Red Riding Hood (op cit, pages 64-68) and used them to explain how people respond emotionally. He used these stories to help people understand the psychological games people play in life.

Little Red Riding Hood games

If possible, the therapist gets hold of a soft toy Little Red Riding Hood, especially one that can transform into the wolf and grandmother. Depending on the age of the client they encourage the child or children to consider the strategies or games everyone plays in life:

■ *What mother would send an innocent girl alone into the woods?*
■ *What grandmother would invite a wolf into her house?*
■ *How could Riding Hood mix up the wolf for her grandmother?*
■ *How could the wolf dare to imagine it would get away with being grandmother?*

Therapeutic purpose: Little Red Riding Hood and other traditional stories, which usually have a sinister element, enable children and young people to explore and come to terms with 'darker' parts of their self.

The child's own story

In therapy, stories can be used to help children understand themselves and make internal script changes. For instance, the therapist might read a story and the child then does a drawing based on the story. With assistance from the therapist the resulting drawing tells the child something about themselves. Child clients can then decide whether they are happy with the result or want to make a script change.

Another way of exploring the child's or young person's own story is to scatter around the counselling room a selection of pictures taken from magazines. The client is invited to walk around looking at as many of them as they can. Then the counsellor suggests that they choose a picture (or more than one picture), find a quiet place and write their story as if they were the character in the picture – an animal, a person, a house or even a tree. They are encouraged to write in the first person (I, me etc) and in the present tense 'I am going . . .' etc). They can spend up to 20 minutes writing the story.

Once the story or part of it is written down, the child or young person is encouraged to read it out loud (or speak it out loud if it is a picture). The therapist then listens without interruption or interpretation. Of course, the young client may want to bring their own interpretation, which is fine. Reading the story and being listened to with respect, and without interruption, can be therapeutic in itself. And the message of the story can be self-healing.

Later, the child or young person and counsellor can discuss the story if the client wants to. Be aware, even at this stage, to listen to what the client thinks and feels without the counsellor imposing their own views.

Younger children who don't yet have the ability to write a story could draw it or explain it to the therapist.

NOTE: If the counsellor is doing this activity in a training context as a way of understanding the process, they may find it difficult to choose a picture using their intuition without *thinking too much about it. One of the big differences between adults and children is that children choose intuitively 'just because', whereas adults think, reason and consider. Our advice is: Simply use intuition, letting the picture choose you. Then use that same intuition as you write.*

Therapeutic purpose: The Child's Own Story is about exploring the young client's internal processes, enabling the child or young person to express what is going on for them through a story.

The six-year-old client chose every animal figure he could find, including snakes and lizards, then sat as close as he could to the therapist. 'Let's be brothers and start a pet shop,' he said.

As his story developed he made pretend drinks for himself and the therapist, then put wet sand in stacking cups as food for them both. At times he just wanted to sit peacefully beside the therapist, eating and drinking together. At the end of the story he appeared happier and more relaxed.

It seemed to the therapist that the young client was using an acted-out story to heal his past, which had included possible abuse and abandonment by an adult figure in his life.

Visualisation

Creative visualisation enables young clients to explore their own processes and perhaps make new decisions about how they are going to be in life. In TA terms this sorting out of emotional difficulties is called a script change.

Dr Eric Berne, founder of TA, introduced to the therapy world the concept of script (or life-script). He defined script as 'an ongoing life plan formed in early childhood under parental pressure. It is the psychological force which propels the person toward his destiny, regardless of whether he fights it or says it is his own free will' (Berne, 1972/1975, page 52). Stewart & Joines (1987) refine this definition as 'an unconscious life-plan made in childhood, reinforced by the parents, "justified" by subsequent events, and culminating in a chosen alternative' (page 330).

As children we make our own script decisions at an unconscious level as the best way we know at the time for responding to the world around us. Those script decisions were useful at the time but some of them now restrict our clients, including child clients, in their relationships, emotions and attitudes to life.

For making new script decisions, one of the most powerful and useful creative visualisations that has stood the test of time is John Allan's Rosebush visualisation (Allan, 1988). Here is one of the many adapted versions used in therapy with children, young people and even adults:

The rosebush

Close your eyes and imagine you are a rosebush. Become that rosebush now. (PAUSE)

What kind of rosebush are you? Are you small . . . large . . . wide . . .tall? (PAUSE) Do you have flowers? What kind? What are your stems and branches like? Do you have thorns? (PAUSE) What are your roots like? . . . Or maybe you don't have any. If you have roots, are they long and straight? Are they twisted? Deep? (PAUSE)

Look around you. Are you in a garden? In a park? In the desert? In the city? In the country? In the middle of the sea? In a pot or growing on the ground, or through the cement? (PAUSE) Look around you. What do you see? Other flowers?

Are you alone? Are there any trees? (PAUSE) Animals? (PAUSE) People? (PAUSE) Birds? (PAUSE)

Do you look like a rosebush or something else? (PAUSE) Is there a fence around you? (PAUSE) Does someone take care of you? (PAUSE)

What's the weather like for you right now? What is your life like? How do you feel? (PAUSE) What happens as the seasons change? (PAUSE) Be aware of being a rosebush. Look carefully. (PAUSE)

In a minute I will ask you to open your eyes and to draw or paint a picture of yourself as a rosebush. Then I'll ask you to talk about the picture as if you are the rosebush. When you are ready open your eyes and begin your picture. (PAUSE)

Here are some suggested questions to ask and statements to make after the drawing is finished:

- *What kind of rosebush are you, and what do you look like?*
- *Talk about your flowers.*
- *Tell me about about your leaves.*
- *Describe your stems and branches.*
- *Do you have thorns? If so, tell me about them. If not, how do you protect yourself?*
- *Are you a mean or a friendly rosebush?*
- *What are your roots like?*
- *Tell me about where you live.*
- *What kind of things do you see around you?*
- *How do you like living where you are?*
- *Do you think you look like a rosebush, or something else? If so, what?*
- *Who takes care of you?*
- *How do you feel about that?*
- *How do they look after you?*
- *What's the weather like for you right now?*
- *What happens to you as the seasons change?*
- *How does it feel to be a rosebush?*
- *What is your life like as a rosebush?*

Therapeutic purpose: With new personal information through *The Rosebush,* young clients can decide to update or revise their life-script through new decisions. We have also used it as a form of clinical governance, comparing a drawing near the beginning of therapy with one later on; the resulting visual positive change can be startling.

Practicalities

Creative visualisation can help both child and adult clients to make script changes at a deep level. It is a way of forming images in the mind and turning them into signals to the body and emotions. It can be used for relaxation, looking at problems in a different way or seeing life more positively.

Psychotherapy trainer Ian Stewart emphasises the importance of the therapist speaking in a natural way when leading a visualisation. He writes: 'There's no need to use a "goofy voice". Just talk in a natural and relaxed way, at an easy pace. If you are leading the visualisation for just one person (as opposed to a group), you may like to match the pace of her/his breathing, and speak on the out-breath. If you do this, keep it casual – don't attempt to get it exact' (Stewart, 2002).

In a similar way our own approach was very down to earth. We spoke in a normal voice. We gave the option of closing eyes or not and we always included something practical to do after the visualisation: drawing, writing, clay, movement, paint, drama, collage/3D or human sculpting. This helped to anchor the message of the creative visualisation, making it far deeper and more memorable for the young client.

Our book *Stories that Heal: 64 Creative visualisations for use in therapy* (Day & Day, 2011/2014) contains a wealth of further information about using creative visualisations with child, youth and adult clients as well as groups. For now here is one of our own creative visualisations for counsellors to use with their child clients:

Treasure!

Get comfortable and close your eyes if you want. We are going treasure hunting.

You have found a very old map of a tropical island with a large X showing where the treasure is buried. (PAUSE) Your boat has just landed on the beach of the deserted island. (PAUSE) Are you excited? (PAUSE) Anxious? (PAUSE) Relaxed? (PAUSE) Afraid? (PAUSE)

With machete in one hand and spade in the other you find it difficult to hold your map. (PAUSE) You struggle through the undergrowth, cutting a path for yourself, going upwards towards the top of the island. (PAUSE) What can you see? (PAUSE) What can you hear? (PAUSE)

What is it like being in such a hot place? (PAUSE) What do you think about the dangers? (PAUSE) Are you worried about snakes? (PAUSE) Tropical diseases? (PAUSE) Or are you taking life as it comes? (PAUSE)

You notice an outcrop of rock and check your map. (PAUSE) Almost there. (PAUSE) You find a large round stone sticking out of the ground and measure 20 paces from it, as your map shows. (PAUSE) Then you start to dig. (PAUSE) The digging is very difficult because of the many roots. (PAUSE) You hack away with your machete and this helps you to use your spade on the soil. (PAUSE)

After what seems like hours your spade strikes something hard and metallic. (PAUSE) You have found the treasure chest! (PAUSE) You scrape away the soil around it and, with a mighty heave, you lift it out of the ground. (PAUSE) There is a strong padlock keeping it closed. (PAUSE) You bang hard with your spade. (PAUSE) Just when you are about to give up, the padlock breaks. (PAUSE) With some effort you manage to lift the lid. (PAUSE)

There it is. (PAUSE) The treasure you have always wanted. (PAUSE) You reach inside and take out the treasure, putting it in your bag. (PAUSE) Then you return to the beach and back into the boat. (PAUSE)

Your mission has been accomplished. (PAUSE)

Now, climb out of the boat and back into the room. Open your eyes and create your treasure using the art materials here.

Therapeutic purpose: The creative visualisation *Treasure!* Can help children and young people to identify things they really want deep down inside. The treasure they find may be about life changes rather than something material.

Transitional object

Once children or young people have done this visualisation –
or others similar to it – it is often effective to offer a piece of
treasure for the young client to take home.

The item doesn't have to be of any great value. For
instance, the counsellor could collect natural objects from
the woods, parks or beaches – such as acorns, chestnuts or
pebbles – and give them to child, youth or adult clients as
what Donald Winnicott in the early 1950s called 'transitional
objects'.

A transitional object has since been defined as 'an
object used by a child to provide comfort and security while
he or she is away from a secure base, such as mother or
home' (Mosby 1982/2017, page 1793). In this case the
secure base is the therapy room from which the client moves
out into the world beyond.

5
Equal opportunities

Equality is a vital element in working with children and young people. If a therapist is working with children or young people for an organisation or offering their services to a school, for instance, it is important to have an Equal Opportunities Policy. It may seem excessive, routine and not necessary, yet people expect counsellors to have thought through these issues.

Appendix B contains an outline Equal Opportunities Policy that counsellors and organisations are welcome to use and can adapt for their use.

Much of the wording might not apply if the counsellor is working alone. Yet having the full policy in place makes it easier to take on other counselling and administrative staff in the future should the work expand.

The policy also needs to reflect the way a counsellor treats child and adolescent clients. Discrimination is not acceptable in any of its many forms. This does not mean that a counsellor must accept and work with every client. Indeed, as the counsellor progresses in their work with young clients, it is likely to become increasingly clear what client groups they are unwilling to work with because of insufficient experience or training. This, however, is very different from refusing a client simply because of bias against them.

The policy will need to be reviewed and updated on a regular basis. Such reviews must take into account changes in society. For instance, at the time of writing, there is considerable discussion about gender issues in children. Questions for discussion on future policy changes might include discrimination around the areas of gender realignment and gender neutrality in children. Professionals are divided between seeing this as an important right for any child or seeing the provision of gender-changing hormones to young children as a form of child abuse.

Are these valid areas to include in a future policy or are they passing fads? Only time will tell.

6
Puppets

Hand puppets are extremely useful in counselling children and particularly teenagers. They enable both child and adolescent clients to express parts of their personality that are normally difficult to access.

Puppets have a long and distinguished history. They seem to have originated in several different countries. Puppet theatre is mentioned in both Aristotle's and Plato's writings. Some puppets were tribal ritual masks with hinged jaws or jointed skulls used in religious ceremonies. Then doll-like figures with moving limbs were developed. Native Americans used puppets in their festivals and dances. Egyptians made jointed puppets from terracotta.

Thousands of years ago China introduced shadow puppets from the stretched, translucent skin of donkeys, sheep, water buffaloes, pigs or fish. They were placed in front of a screen with light passing through it. The shadows appeared clearly to the audience on the other side.

Turkish puppeteers added waist movement to their shadow puppets and began controlling-rod arm movements from the side, rather than the bottom, as the Chinese had done.

In The Middle Ages the Christian church used puppets to spread the Christian message. The Nativity – the story of the birth of Jesus – was a favourite play. The puppets used were marionettes, small jointed figures operated with strings. The name Marionette, meaning 'Little Mary', may have come from the figure of the Virgin Mary, Mother of Jesus, in the telling of the Nativity story. Today marionettes are widely used throughout the world, though they aren't popular in the therapy room.

In the 14th or 15th century puppeteers began to explore other themes, including comedy. The church decided puppets were no longer suitable for their teaching. Puppets found a new home in the streets and fairs of the working class. By the sixteenth century, puppet theatres existed all over Europe.

In the 17th century, puppets with heads and a body of cloth that fitted over the puppeteer's hand became popular. These hand puppets (the ones with finger parts are called glove puppets) were easier to use and cheaper to make. They were popular for commenting on local politics. Political shows using hand puppets, such as Punch and Judy, still exist in the UK.

Hand or glove puppets are the most useful puppets in therapy with children and young people. Puppets of animal figures are often the most effective because children and teenagers can create a wide variety of characters out of just one animal figure.

The Sunniebunniezz website has written about using puppets:

'It is still one of the safest ways to act out, act up, entertain, educate, commiserate, wonder out loud, unburden yourself or release your feelings. I have used it, along with my story telling, to fulfil my need to see the good guys win and justice done. It has always been both a sword and a shield to me. It is my armour in a world of frustrations and disappointments, when indeed, the bad [people] seem to be ahead in this game we call Life. In short, I have found Puppet Theatre to be a wonderful place to find peace of mind and spirit' (Sunniebunniezz, 2017).

Puppets can be used therapeutically to:
- *Show empathy*
- *Make connection.*
- *Express emotions.*
- *Explore new possibilities.*
- *Become free from the past.*
- *Role play the child's or teenager's own problems.*
- *Comfort.*
- *Understand.*

Ideally, both the therapist and the young person are involved in using puppets in the therapy session. When working with puppets it is important to be sincere. The counsellor needs to maintain eye contact with the puppet, not the client, and – for instance – offer a tissue to the puppet if the puppet seems upset.

Finding a voice

The first step in working with puppets in counselling is to choose puppets. The therapist invites the child or young people to choose a puppet and get to know the puppet. At the same time the counsellor also chooses a puppet. The client finds the puppet's voice and practises saying hello using their puppet. The counsellor also finds a voice for their puppet. In both cases the puppet's voice is inevitably different from their own voice. Then in turns they introduce their puppet using the puppet's voice.

Therapeutic purpose: Finding a Voice enables the young client to explore another part of their personality that isn't generally seen. It can be quite a surprise when the puppet is such a different personality from the client!

Bullying

Experience shows that puppets can be very useful in helping children and young people who are being bullied by other children or intimidated by adults.

The therapist introduced puppets to a 13-year-old boy. As the boy played with them he wanted the counsellor involved. Suddenly the boy had an idea. He had been physically abused and humiliated by his mother's boyfriend. His idea was that the therapist's puppet played the part of the boy and his would be the boyfriend, this evil stepfather. As they played with their puppets together, suddenly the client's puppet became really vicious. The therapist realised that this had now become real. The counsellor had to make sure their puppet (the client) won. If they didn't, how could their client ever know that the therapist could protect him?

Finally, after a very physical fight between the two puppets, the therapist won with their puppet, representing the boy. Normally the therapist would have eased back on the fight so that the client had a good chance of winning. In this case it seemed important for the therapist to win.

The client, with the therapist's help, thinks of a puppet scenario in which a child has experienced bullying. Once the child/young person and therapist have the scenario, they work out a script for helping the child who is being bullied. Then the child and counsellor practise the scene using the puppets. Once the scene has been performed, the therapist gives time to discuss what was presented.

Similar puppet scenarios can be made about feelings: scare, anger, sadness and joy.

Therapeutic purpose: Exploring *Bullying* using puppets can enable young clients to contact feelings about bullying and learn strategies for dealing with any bullying in their lives. The same applies to exploring one or more of the various emotions.

Puppets with families and groups

Puppets have been proved useful in family therapy. When various family members use puppets they tend to take on distinct roles that may be similar to those in the family. Children and adults seem to enjoy them. Surprisingly so do most teenagers when they get used to the idea. Teenagers especially like the humour they can use through puppets. The therapist is advised to ensure they have some rules for teenagers so things don't get too much out of hand.

In this exercise some interesting things come out when the children or family members hide behind something – a bit like a theatre – so that only the puppets are showing. In this setting the puppets become responsible for their own work and action. There can be some quite dramatic results using this approach.

Whether working in a family or therapy group, the instruction is similar:

Please develop a puppet play in which only the puppets appear. I won't see your faces. Use the puppets to express an emotion you don't normally show in public. Examples are happy, sad, angry, scared. Then let the other puppets respond. You can also use your puppets to say things to the rest of the audience. The simple rules are: 'Respect other people' and 'Use only words that are socially acceptable'.

Therapeutic purpose: The activity *Puppets with Families and Groups* enables counsellor and client to look at what is happening at a psychology rather than just a social level within the family system or therapy group.

Theoretical understanding

Puppets can be understood theoretically in a number of different ways. The hand 'costume' of a hand puppet can stimulate fantasy play. It can also be what Donald Winnicott (1960) called a 'holding environment'. In the inner darkness of the puppet secrets can be safe after the child has whispered them into the puppet's ear or the puppet has whispered them into the child's ear.

Gudrun Gaudas writes: 'The indirect work with puppets create a *safe space for self-exploration,* lessening its eventual threatening impact. It is not me, but instead the puppet that is doing things, things I might never dare to do ... In the safe space the client apart from this can develop the ability for *symbolisation*, the nonverbal can become verbal as the stories unfold. The client is helped by feeling a sense of *self-control;* he/she is in many ways in charge of the puppets. Since the puppet making and playing requires working with different degrees of control and frustration tolerance, he/she can also get some training in this' (Gaudas, 2017).

Farryl Hadari writes: 'When the puppeteer personifies the puppet, he facilitates the creation of a psychological distance between the puppet and the puppeteer and between the puppeteer and the audience. This distance enables the puppeteer to step back to a *safe place* where he can examine behaviour, opinions, emotions and reactions. The therapist can join in these reflections, which can provide a path for intervention. Intervention is an interference of involvement in a situation with the goal of modifying or altering a process in the situation' (Hadari, 2017).

Transactional analysis uses the term 'ego states'. 'An ego state is a set of related behaviours, thoughts and feelings' (Stewart & Joines, 1987, page 4). When a person responds to what is going on in the here and now, using all their resources, they are in Adult ego state. When they act, think or feel in the way parent figures acted towards them they are in Parent. When they return to behaving, thinking and feeling in the way they did as a child of a particular age they are in Child ego state.

The use of puppets can be seen as a way for the young person out of awareness to contact their Child ego state at a certain age or stage in order to make changes. Puppets enable a person to deal with uncomfortable things in the past in a way that is socially acceptable.

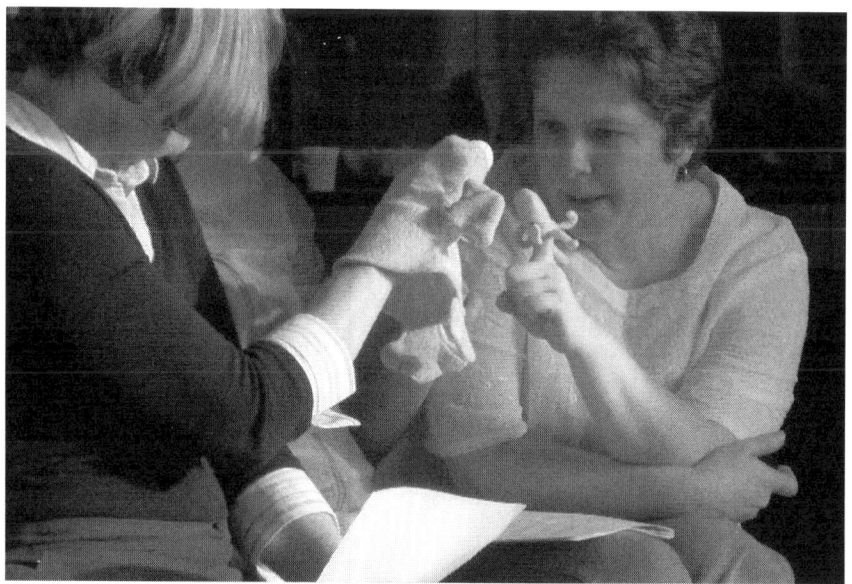

7
Child observation

The counsellor wanting to start working with children, young people and families is strongly advised to take part in a *child observation* exercise, writing up their results and discussing them with their specialist supervisor or another counsellor experienced in working with clients under the age of 16.

The main purpose of this observation is to watch how a small child or toddler plays and interacts with the adults around them. The intention is to watch what is considered 'normal' play and gain a better understanding of the way a young child learns to play and communicate. Hopefully this is what the counsellor will see during their observation.

The ideal involves watching (with parents' permission where possible) specific children at play *in various settings* over a period of time (at least six weeks). It could be a child of the counsellor's friend, for instance. This will include at least one observation of a parent, grandparent or carer playing with a small child or baby. Thoughts and comments about the play observation are then written up in the form of a report.

The child observation is not intended as a way for the therapist to criticise parenting skills or comment on problems they notice in the child. They are not to become a 'therapist' or 'adviser' during the course of the observation. By seeing normal development of play it will hopefully help the counsellor to notice the play of child clients and see areas of concern when their play does not fit with a normal, or usual, healthy pattern.

Generally the counsellor doesn't participate in the play, though some children will want this to happen and invite the counsellor into their play. This is not intended as a serious, heavy task. It can be fun for everyone.

What to look for

In observing play it is important to look for examples of pretend and role play. This will include how children use items around them as well as the setting (the room, the playground or the garden) in which they create a game using just imagination.

The observation also involves looking for ways in which children use play to help resolve their problems as well as developing rules in their play. Do they get messy or not? Do parents, grandparents and carers interact in the play or not? In group games do the observed children join in or do they stay out of the group?

Background information on observing play

The following notes may be useful when the counsellor plans their observation of play and in writing their report based on their observation:

1. Functions of play
Children see play as having a number of functions:

- *Fun.*
- *Learning to do new things.*
- *Interesting.*
- *Getting to know people.*
- *Role playing.*
- *Experimenting.*

2. Reasons for play
One early-years assessment team gives the reasons for play as follows:

- *Play is a natural means of expression for most children.*
- *Play provides a natural and appealing setting.*

- *Play allows children to experience a wide number of emotions and situations.*
- *Play is a child-initiated and child-maintained activity.*
- *Play is a tool for learning*
- *Play is flexible and should not be intrusive to the child's pre-school experience.*
- *Play helps adults to understand how children approach tasks, thereby offering ways of improving their learning.*

3. Types of play

Kenneth Rubin (1989) classifies play observation as follows:

- **Social play.**
    Solitary play.
    Parallel play.
    Group play.

- **Cognitive play.**
    Functional play.
    Constructive play.
    Dramatic play.
    Games with rules.

- **Non-play activities.**
    Exploratory.
    Reading.
    Unoccupied behaviour.
    Onlooker behaviour.
    Transition.
    Active conversation.
    Aggression.
    Rough-and-tumble.

4. Guidelines on child observation

Here are some ideas from a college course in which students observed children at play:

Use the information you gathered while observing as evidence to support the claims you make about the child:

■ *Discuss whether or not the child demonstrated the types of play you would expect for their age, and explain why or why not.*
■ *Based on the activities that you observed analyse what you can about one or two areas of the child's development such as personality, emotions, language, physical, and/or cognitive areas.*
■ *If possible, include any contextual (based on the current environment), biological (what you can tell visibly), and/or interactional influences that may contribute to this child's play and social interactions.*
■ *Interpret the dynamics you noticed among the group. Discuss any observation you made about age or gender affecting the way children play.*
■ *Conclude by summarising benefits the child may gain from the play you observed, and/or providing suggestions for future activities or materials. You may express your opinion of this observation experience and any questions that remain for you about the importance of children's play to their overall development.*

5. Play observation – an example
The following example of play observation was published anonymously by an American university student:

I decided to conduct my play observation at the child studies centre here on campus. I observed a number of different groups of children at different times, in various areas of the centre. Generally, there were about two to four children engaging in a play activity at a given time. The approximate ages of the children I paid close attention to ranged from three to five years of age.

Each play segment lasted about 10 to 15 minutes in length, with the outdoors portion lasting about 20 minutes. I tried to vary the areas of play so I could get a good idea of what went on in different environments, with various activities and varied toys. I viewed a couple of different groups and types of play going on at the same time, in separate areas of the classroom, during the free play period.

First, I witnessed a little girl wearing a blanket tied around her neck, representing a cape, participating in solitary isolated and symbolic play. She did, however, run up to me, place a miniature tree on the table I was sitting at, gave me a smile and ran away. In another instance, three children were playing on a computer sitting side by side, not talking to one another, completely engrossed in their games. One teacher attempted, on several occasions, to persuade the boys to leave the computers and go make a craft (not art!) with a group of the other children. It was evident that they had no interest in making crafts and tried to negotiate with the teacher for the infamous 'five more minutes'.

Another little girl was lying on the floor in the same room, near the boys playing on the computer, engaging in onlooker play. In a different area of the classroom, a little girl was playing at the 'house' section, washing dishes and arranging food. Shortly after, another boy came and joined along with the girl in associative play. From what I noticed about the play type, the two were engaging in sociodramatic play, acting as if they were married. The girl gave the boy a piece of fake food, to which he responded, 'Thank you, dear.'

A few of the older boys, about four and five, were quite rowdy and didn't pay attention to the teacher when asked to stop. They grabbed a long hose and started yanking it around the room, carelessly. One boy exclaimed, 'Let go of the hose! Please,' which of course just made the other boys continue. I don't think they were participating in any type of play so much as they were trying to cause trouble in the classroom.

During the outdoor free play portion of my observation, children split up into small groups, and participated in a variety of activities such as riding tricycles around, swinging on the swing set, playing in and on the playground equipment, and engaging in make-believe play.

Through observing the children at play, from a bystander perspective, armed with my knowledge about types and levels of play from class, it was interesting to watch all the different kinds of play that transpired. After observing the children at play, I would make sure that for my future classroom practice, having the supplies and toys available to foster various types and levels of play in children would be a top priority.

I learned from this experience that children engage in a wide variety of play, but mostly gravitate towards solitary isolated, associative and cooperative play. I did not witness any unoccupied behaviour going on at all during my hour visit. Children are naturally curious and by having the resources available and in front of children will naturally gravitate towards items that they can play with in some way. They might not even use the toy how it was intended, and that can be a wonderful outcome in and of itself, building upon the endless possibilities of children's creativity.

Play is a great way to expand children's emotional, social, physical and intellectual development all at one time, while giving them the freedom of enjoyment and mastery of their own feelings.

8
Sandtray

Introduction

Sandtray is one of the most powerful approaches and is vital in work with many children and young people. That is one of the reasons why we are including plenty of theory about it in this section. Be aware, though, that a few young clients may not like the feel of sand or the mess it makes. These could include those on the autistic spectrum and others with sensory issues.

Think of sandtray as a way of tapping into the unconscious processes of the child or young person in a similar way to how our brains use dreams to sort things out and resolve problems while we are asleep.

Sandtray is now used extensively with adults. However, it was originally developed for use with children, based partly on the playwright H G Wells and the floor games he developed with his two small sons using toys (Wells, 1912/2004). In the 1930s paediatrician Margaret Lowenfeld introduced two zinc trays of sand and a box of small toys and other small objects into her consulting room. Children began referring to these items as their world. As a result, Lowenfeld coined the phrase World Technique to describe her sandtray work.

Twenty years later Dora Kalff moved to the UK to study under Lowenfeld. She took the ideas she learned and combined them with eastern philosophy, Neuman's system model and Carl Jung's archetypes and theory of individuation. What emerged was a technique that she described as sandplay therapy. Ever since then, *sandplay* has referred to a Jungian approach and *sandtray* is applied to all other models. In this book we use the more generic word *sandtray.*

The small objects could be used on their own, which then becomes known as 'small world'. The sand adds a different dimension that is often natural to the child or young person and also represents the person's unconscious processes. People have described sandtray therapy as a kind of daytime dream.

Most adults naturally create a still picture in the sandtray. Children, however, tend to create a dynamic sandtray that is constantly moving. Some of the books on sandtray and sandplay show photographs of sandtrays with a small hand moving objects as the picture is being taken! Some children will produce a static sandtray but many won't. It is important for note-taking to take a picture of each sandtray (more than one if it keeps changing). This can then be discussed in supervision. With children making dynamic sandtrays it may be a case of getting a picture whenever possible, even if it shows a child's hand still at work.

Usually the child or young person can be shown the sandtray and objects and simply invited to create what they like. Sometimes, though, it is useful to give direction to the client. Both approaches are valid. There is more on this subject in our popular book *Creative Therapy in the Sand: Using sandtray with clients* (Day, 2012a).

Be aware that much of the work in sandtray is at a very deep level. The child may need to repeat a sandtray many times, making tiny changes, before they are ready to move on. On the other hand, the therapist may find that a child or young person does one sandtray and then refuses to do any more. Intuitively the client knows they don't want to go any deeper. It is important to respect the young person's intuition in this area.

Rubberbanding

Before looking at a therapy activity involving sandtray we want to introduce a theoretical concept that is known as 'rubberbanding', which comes from TA (transactional analysis).

A rubberband has been defined as 'a point of similarity between a here-and-now stress situation and a painful situation from the person's own childhood, usually not recalled in awareness, in response to which the person is likely to go into script' (Stewart & Joines, 1987, page 333).

The effect can be clearly understood by taking a literal rubberband and, with great care, stretch it and allow it to snap back. It returns to its original point and often goes even further, causing some discomfort

This is an illustration of what sometimes happens in creative therapy. Child and teenage clients carry forward from any major experience in their past something like a rubberband that when a crisis comes draws them suddenly back to that original experience and their response to it at the time. Often they don't remember that original experience and it comes as a surprise. They just snap back to it. The counsellor needs to be ready in case this happens in sandtray work or using other creative techniques. Otherwise it could cause something of a shock!

It is useful to have some rubberbands available in family or group work to illustrate this to the adults and older children.

Commenting on feelings

Often it is useful to let the child or young person do exactly what they want (within reason) with the objects in the sandtray, while the counsellor observes. This doesn't mean that there aren't any rules. We recommend simple rules like keeping the sand in the sandtray and respecting the objects being used and the people in the room.

The process of *Commenting on Feelings* involves inviting the young client to choose some objects and place them in the sandtray.

It is important to watch the face of the client as they choose, not just look at the objects being chosen. The same applies when the client places of the objects in the sandtray. This takes quite a lot of practice because naturally the focus is on the hands and the objects being used.

A rule for the therapist is that only the client touches the objects. As the process continues, the counsellor may notice on the client's face indications of an emotion. In the exercise *Commenting on Feelings* the therapist then simply states what emotion they think they have noticed without any further comment. For instance: 'You seem happy', or 'You look sad'.

When the client has finished the counsellor asks two or three times questions such as: 'Are you finished?' 'Are you sure?' 'Is there anything else you need to do?' When they are sure that the client has finished, the counsellor asks them what it was like. It is important to avoid analysis or interpretation.

Therapeutic purpose: By the counsellor identifying emotions and *Commenting on Feelings* the young client will begin to understand and react to the emotions that they are facing as they work in the sandtray. Further therapeutic work on feelings can then be planned (see chapter 16).

What I want my world to be like

Another sandtray that child and adolescent clients could create is called *What I Want My World to be Like*. As the child works in the sandtray the counsellor watches their facial expressions and (out of the corner of the eye) the objects that are placed in the tray. It is too distracting to comments while the sandtray is progressing.

When the task is completed the counsellor asks the young person about their sandtray. Here is a chance for the therapist to be curious without imposing ideas on the client. They might ask questions:

■ *Talk about your sandtray.*
■ *Tell me about what you've made.*

The counsellor with a well-developed intuition may be drawn to a particular object or series of objects. They simply say:

■ *Tell me about this.*

They avoid touching the object or identifying it in any way verbally, because what looks like a cat to the counsellor may represent a parent to the child.

Therapeutic purpose: Enabling the young client to visualise a positive future. Providing an opportunity for the therapist to use intuition in assessing their young client's sandtray. The activity *What I Want My World to be Like* can also be used as a way of contracting with the client (see chapter 11).

Dreams and wishes

The type of sandtray described above helps the child or adolescent client to use creative imagination in moving out of their current difficulties into a happier place. Children – and adults, for that matter – love stories where good triumphs over evil. This sandtray is not just fantasy; some of it can become a reality for the child, however difficult their circumstances.

Eric Berne, the founder of TA, used two expressions to describe the human desire to move out of the present difficulties into a positive future. The first was the Greek term *physis*. This could be defined as 'the energy for growth present in all living beings'. It fits well with one of the three TA philosophical statements: 'People decide their own destiny, and these decisions can be changed' Stewart & Joines, 1987, page 6). Child clients have already made script decisions or are in the process of making them. Physis enables them to grow and change those decisions when they are ready.

The other expression Berne used for growth and change was the Aspiration Arrow. Petruska Clarkson wrote that the aspiration arrow 'represents the dynamic force of Physis' (Clarkson, 1992, page 13).

The Aspiration Arrow rises above and outside the ego states, implying that it is entering the transpersonal or spiritual realm. It is important in therapy with children and young people to allow them to explore this spiritual realm for themselves.

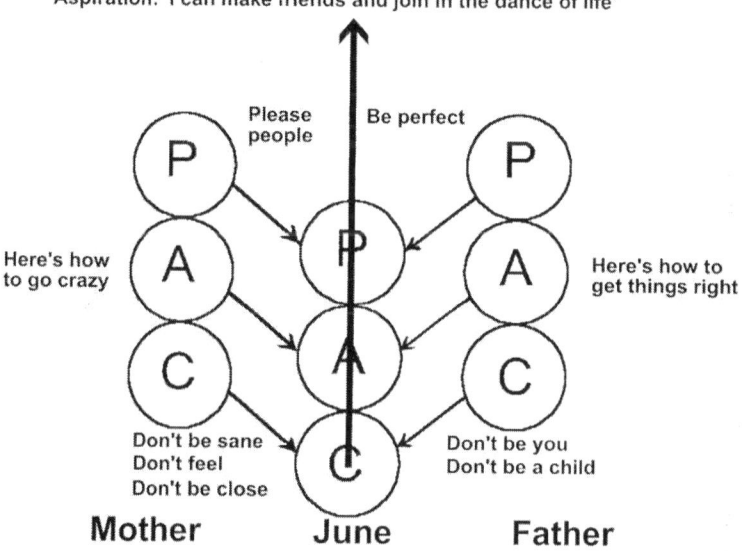

Diagram C2: Script matrix (Berne, 1972/75b, after Steiner, 1966)

My family

This final sandtray, *My Family,* is different from the others mentioned above because, rather than an individual, it is sandtray therapy with the whole family – children and adults. The family does the sandtray together, concentrating on their section without paying much attention to the others. It can also work with a group of young clients who have worked together for some time and know each other well.

When they have all finished, they stand back from the sandtray and look at what they've created. They can be invited to move around to see the sandtray from different angles. They are then asked to start discussing together what they observe.

Then the family members talk about any changes they would like to make in the sandtray that could help the family represented in the sandtray to function better together. After making the changes they look again, making more changes if necessary until they have finished.

Therapeutic purpose: My Family enables the whole family to explore their own family system visually (or a similar exploration for a group of young clients who know each other well). By doing so, hopefully they are able to identify areas within their family life that may need changing.

The family consisted of mother, father and two teenage girls. They had attended several sessions of counselling that they found reasonably helpful. There was something else that seemed unresolved though no one in the family – or even the therapist – could identify what it was. The therapist therefore suggested a family sandtray.

When they had finished the sandtray they stood back and looked. Did it represent their family? They shook their heads and started again.

This time they created a series of hand prints in the sandtray of varying sizes. They also searched the sandtray objects more thoroughly. At the very bottom of one of the boxes they came across some pieces of a toy person that had once been held together with elastic. Intuitively they partly buried these in the sand quite near to each other.

This time they stood back and looked again, all nodding their heads with plenty of enthusiasm. Yes, this was their family recreated in the sandtray.

'What's made the difference?' the counsellor asked, intrigued.

'It's something to do with those pieces of the person we put into the sand.'

'Any idea what it could mean?'

'The broken man,' said one of the girls suddenly. The rest said yes to this.

'The broken man?' asked the therapist.

'It's my husband,' said the mother through tears. 'Ever since he had his stroke he's like a different person, and none of us realised that until just now.'

Family systemic approach

When working with a family in therapy it is important to look at the whole system rather than just the individuals within it. The above sandtray is one of several ways of using sandtray to give families the chance to heal their own structure. One definition of family systemic therapy is as follows:

Systemic therapy neither attempts a 'treatment of causes' nor of symptoms, rather it gives living systems nudges that help them to develop new patterns together, taking on a new organisational structure that allows growth (Schlippe & Schweitzer, 1998, page 93).

A useful (though expensive) book that contains further information on family sandtray is Lois Carey's *Sandtray Therapy with Children and Families* (Carey, 1999).

9
Transferring skills

Introduction

The qualified counsellor with experience in working with adults already has many of the needed skills. These can be transferred to working with children, young people and families. It is important for the counsellor to remember that they are *qualified* as a counsellor. They are *not* a trainee or student counsellor and can charge for their work with children if they want to.

In addition to the counsellor qualification/s and having a theoretical and practical grasp of working with children, the counsellor will need the following:

1. Professional membership

It is vital to be a member of a professional counselling organisation and willing to abide by that organisation's ethical guidelines. Many organisations have subsections within them for people specialising as children's counsellors, and it is probably a good idea to join these as well. These often offer a specialist magazine and provide details of extra training in working with children and young people.

2. Specialist supervision

A supervisor is needed who specialises in therapy with children, young people, families or creative therapy. The counsellor could talk to their current supervisor and see if they are willing to provide such specialist supervision. If not, they might consider keeping their existing supervision arrangements and seeing another supervisor for the element of their work with young clients. If there is no suitable supervisor in the counsellor's local area or within reasonable commuting distance, an arrangement using Skype or FaceTime is possible, though bear in mind that creative supervision using sandtray and other means will then not be as effective. This supervision ideally will start with several sessions before seeing the first child.

3. Police check

A police check must be in place before the therapist starts seeing the first child or young person. The process for this varies from country to country. A simple search for 'police check' in the specific country will enable the counsellor to start the process.

In England and Wales the police check is made through the Disclosure & Barring Service (DBS):

https://www.gov.uk/government/organisations/disclosure-and-barring-service

The person working with people under the age of 16 will need an *enhanced disclosure,* which is not available to a private individual direct from DBS. If the work with children and young people is in an organisation, such as a school, church or counselling agency, the check can be done through them. If not, there are a number of independent agencies that can arrange this for an individual. An internet search will show the agencies providing DBS enhanced searches and the cost of each as a comparison.

If the therapist works with children/young people in more than one organisation (such as a school) they will probably require a fresh DBS check for each place in which they work.

4. Parental permission

It is essential that the therapist has written permission for the therapy from the parent or guardian before they have the first session alone with the child.

The only exceptions in English and Welsh law are in cases where the person under 16 is judged to be 'Gillick Competent' (able to make decisions as if they were over 16). In 1980 Victoria Gillick, a Catholic mother of 10 children (five of them girls), fought for the right to be told if one of her young daughters was given contraceptive advice. She lost the case and in 1983 a legal precedence term came into being, *Gillick Competence.* Under this the professional can withhold information if he or she judges that the young person is able to make informed consent without the need for parental permission or consent.

This is rare but it is useful to know about. Roger worked with a young couple when the girl was 15 and her mother demanded to know what was being discussed. We took legal advice and withheld the information because we judged her to be Gillick Competent.

It is unlikely that a client under the age of, say, 13 would be considered Gillick Competent. Good practice is to invite the parent or guardian to a meeting with the child present to discuss the therapy. Often at this meeting the written permission from the parent can be obtained without having to judge whether or not a young person is Gillick Competent.

5. Confidentiality

The counsellor also needs some sort of agreement with the parent or guardian about *confidentiality.* There are certain exceptions to this, such as when working with children in care.

Unless the child is considered Gillick Competent (see above), the parent or guardian has the right to know what is said and done in the therapy room. Most parents at that first meeting will agree to respect their child's right to confidentiality. However, the counsellor cannot guarantee complete confidentiality to the child. Nor can they use the word 'secret', which is often the word used by abusers.

One way of explaining confidentiality to the child at the first session is to say something like: 'What we do here is just between you and me. I might have to break that rule if you are going to hurt yourself or hurt someone else in a big way, or if someone is hurting you. Your parents might also want to know what we do here and if they ask I will have to tell them. You can decide how much you want to say to them. For example, you could just say something like: We did art today.'

5. What equipment will I need?

Adults generally work through their problems with words. Children, on the other hand, generally use play and creativity to solve their difficulties. Young people often fall somewhere between those two approaches. Throughout this book we have given plenty of ideas about play and art items that can be used in working with children and young people. Here is a list of basic items to get the counsellor started:

Paper.
Felt-tip pens.
Pencils.
Glitter, sequins, glue.
A few plastic animals, soldiers, people.
A couple of glove puppets.
A small soft toy or two.
Sandtray.
Play sand.
A few shakers and other simple musical instruments.
A few objects to represent the spiritual such as a small cross or two, an angel and a couple of gems.
Natural objects such as feathers, seeds, leaves and pine cones.

We've included here the absolute basic equipment needed to start. We advise people to buy secondhand where possible. That way children and young people may find it easier to use the equipment in the way they need to (which may be quite roughly at times). A counsellor doesn't have to be rich to be working therapeutically with children.

Appendix D contains a full list of equipment that can be used in a well-equipped therapy room. Please note that it isn't necessary to have the complete list of items before starting. The equipment can be added to as the work with children grows.

6. How do I find child/adolescent clients?

There are a growing number of children and young people with emotional issues and relatively few opportunities for them to work through those difficulties. Statutory therapy services are often stretched to the limit, with long waiting lists.

The counsellor might start by approaching the primary or secondary schools in their area. They could consider local counselling agencies, churches or children's clubs. Some of these may already have a list of children and young people needing therapy.

We also recommend producing a leaflet and/or a business card with the therapist's qualifications and what services they offer, circulating it widely in the local area. This may well lead to the counsellor getting private referrals.

As a qualified counsellor they are not seeking a placement in the normal sense of the word, but if one comes up they might well be advised to consider it.

10
Music

Introduction

For hundreds of years music has been known to soothe, relax and even heal people. Here are three quotes about the healing effect of music:

Music imprints itself on the brain deeper than any other human experience. Music evokes emotion and emotion can bring back memory. Music brings back the feeling of life when nothing else can. – Dr Oliver Sacks, 1933-2015, neurologist, naturalist, science historian, author

Music is therapy. Music moves people. It connects people in ways that no other medium can. It pulls heart strings. It acts as a medicine. – Macklemere, 1983-, American rap artist

Music expresses that which cannot be said and on which it is impossible to be silent. – Victor Hugo, 1802-1885, French poet, novelist and dramatist

This section explores using music in therapy with children and young people. Music can be performed or listened to. The difference between this and music therapy is that the latter is led by a trained musician with therapeutic skills and a qualification in music therapy, while using music in therapy is led by a qualified therapist who may or may not have formal musical training.

Here are some definitions of music in therapy:

❒ *It's a form of healing for children and teenagers living with mental or physical disabilities and sensory processing* disorder, acute and chronic pain, eating disorders, abuse, post-traumatic stress disorder and other difficulties.

❏ Music can be used to improve physical, psychological, cognitive and social functioning.

❏ Listening to music in a relaxed state can allow deep feelings and images to arise.

❏ Using music in a safe and secure space helps release feelings.

❏ Sound and music may help some children to control pain, access their body's healing potential, managing stress and emotional healing.

❏ Regular use of music can produce relaxation and desired changes in emotions, behaviour and physiology.

❏ It can be nonverbal self-expression by clients through creating music themselves in the session.

❏ Using music in therapeutic sessions can achieve therapeutic goals, including helping with motor skills, social/interpersonal development, cognitive development, self-awareness and spiritual enhancement.

A classical and biblical example of this spiritual (or transpersonal) enhancement is when the shepherd boy David brought relief to King Saul's troubled mind through playing the harp:

Whenever the spirit from God came upon Saul, David would take his harp and play. Then relief would come to Saul; he would feel better, and the evil spirit would leave him (I Samuel 16:23).

Percussion

Probably the first sense babies develop in the womb is the sense of *hearing*. Researchers have found that children in the womb hear and respond to sounds around them and even outside the womb. In this section we will look at practical ways for using music, including *Percussion,* in counselling with children, young people and families. Some of the exercises may well reflect back to those prebirth experiences and as such may have a powerful effect on children and teenagers who had difficulties before they were born or around the time of their birth.

All the activities mentioned here are suitable for individual children and young people as well as for groups of children and families.

Here are some suggestions for leading a group of children or an individual child in percussion activities:

Let's think of the musical instruments we've already got – our bodies! What comes to your mind when you think of music produced by our bodies? Most people think of hands.

OK, let's use our hands in some rhythm exercises. Someone start by clapping a rhythm and we'll join in.

Now we'll pass a rhythm around the group. The first person looks at the person next to them, make full eye contact, then claps a rhythm. The second person does the same back then turns to their neighbour, passing the message on, right round the group.

Therapeutic purpose: The use of rhythm and *Percussion* enables young clients to explore deep, out-of-awareness feelings and reactions. It is also effective for fun and enjoyment, creativity and building confidence and self-esteem.

One psychotherapist writes:

Drumming has been a wonderfully successful approach to working with kids who have trouble focusing and connecting with others in a satisfying way. Often, these kids have had so much failure in their lives that they come to identify themselves as being 'no good'. A cycle of negative self-reinforcement occurs, often resulting in low self-esteem, depression, anxiety, anger problems and acting out. The personal power awakened by drumming helps to rebuild a sense of efficacy and self-worth. The repetitive rhythm has a physiologically calming effect. It also builds valuable skills for processing and communicating information, and containing or channelling intense emotions and impulses (Schwarcz, 2017).

Body instruments

The activity *Body Instruments* is focused on getting the child/children to think about how many sounds from parts of their body they can use to produce music or rhythm. It's important to say to children doing this activity: 'Please stay polite!' Polite examples might include the clapping already done, tapping toes and patting cheeks with the mouth slightly open.

When working with a group of children the therapist could get them into a circle and suggest that each person in turn plays a different body sound. Then the others, including the therapist, follow the rhythm of that person. Each person who manages to find a new body instrument would then get a small prize such as a smiley sticker.

Once the round has been completed, the therapist invites anyone to come up with more ideas. Each time a different body instrument is used, the others copy the sound together.

Therapeutic purpose: Confidence building, discovering musical ability, plenty of fun.

Finding an instrument

Many people who want to use music in therapy with children and young people think they have to spend lots of money on drums, flutes, whistles and percussion. This isn't strictly true. In addition to percussion instruments already in the room the counsellor and the client can make musical instruments virtually free of charge.

Finding an Instrument involves the therapist inviting the client as 'homework' between sessions to find objects that could be used as musical instruments. Many everyday objects – empty plastic boxes, elastic bands, stones, strips of wood – can become improvised musical instruments.

Whether working with one child or a group of children, they can be invited to perform music with their found instrument. In a group, everyone is invited to have a turn, then clients and therapist play together as an orchestra of 'found sound'.

Therapeutic purpose: Creativity, improvising, imagination, building confidence.

Musical activities

Children and teenagers in therapy may use musical instruments on their own and in the way they want. An alternative is for the therapist to engage the child/children in using the musical instruments in a therapeutic way. It is usually helpful for the young client if the counsellor also takes part in creating music – if the client wants that to happen.

The counsellor could take the lead, inviting young clients to choose a musical instrument that appeals to them. If two people in a group choose the same instrument, the therapist can suggests that they negotiate who uses it first. Clients can be encouraged whenever they like to swap the instrument they have chosen with any other unused instrument. If they prefer to use the instrument they found or one they made, that's OK, too.

Here are some suggested activities:

Introductions
Each person in turn takes part in *Introductions* playing their musical instrument to the other/s with a simple tune or rhythm. After a minute the others join in with the rhythm the person has introduced.

Therapeutic purpose: Listening skills, hand/eye coordination, building confidence, leadership skills.

Follow my lead

In *Follow My Lead* the leader stands in the middle of the group playing a drum or other favoured instrument. Others follow their rhythm. If they play loud, everyone plays loud. If they play soft, everyone plays soft. If they stop, everyone stops. The first leader then chooses the next leader. This continues until everyone who wants to has had a turn at being the leader.

Therapeutic purpose: Concentration, hand-eye coordination, increasing self-esteem, fun.

Mexican wave

The counsellor reminds the children/young people about a *Mexican Wave* at a football match. It starts one side and sweeps across to the other. They then invite the young clients to do that using rhythm. One person starts the wave with their musical instrument, then the next person picks it up. Soon after it has passed them each person stops playing until it comes back to them again. The idea is to keep going round the circle a few times.

Therapeutic purpose: Cooperation, focus, team-building, plenty of fun.

Playing with emotion

Playing with Emotion is a very powerful activity involving feelings. Before starting this activity, the therapist explains about emotions and invites participants to respect each other and give space for the full expression of the person's emotion.

The counsellor starts by calling out an emotion and everyone plays their instrument in a way that expresses that emotion. Someone else is then invited to choose an emotion and take the lead.

If anyone becomes stuck for ideas the therapist could suggest excited, happy, angry, scared or sad.

Therapeutic purpose: Empathy, care, teamwork, expressing real emotions in a safe environment.

The client had foetal alcohol syndrome and resulting uncontrolled behaviour similar to ADHD. The sessions therefore were often chaotic and noisy. One week the client noticed the musical instruments and picked up a small tambourine. He looked over at the counsellor, who took this as an invitation to reflect the client's activity. Without another tambourine he chose a harmonica. He thought it would make a vaguely similar noise. The client shook his tambourine. The counsellor imitated the rhythm on the harmonica. Then the client ran round the room, stopped and again made eye contact. He played a different rhythm and the counsellor reflected it back.

The process went on in a similar fashion for over half the session, the client speeding up the running round the room in an excited way.

At last the client stopped, smiled and put down the tambourine. He had used music to form a link with the therapist, and his emotions had begun to calm down in the sessions. Outside the sessions it was reported that his chaotic behaviour in his adoptive home was slowly improving.

Dedications

The *activity Dedications* is another potentially powerful and emotional way of using musical instruments. The therapist suggests to the client: 'You can dedicate a rhythm to an animal, a house or a person, then chose three people to accompany you in the rhythm.' When they have finished their dedication another person can dedicate a rhythm to someone or something.

Therapeutic purpose: Expressing gratitude in a musical way, teambuilding, learning empathy for team members, enabling emotional expression.

Magic conductor

Magic Conductor is a fun activity ideal for a group of younger children, especially those who have low confidence. One person controls the group's rhythms with a conductor's baton (such as a single chopstick). When it is held high, everyone plays loudly. When it is low, everyone plays softly. When it is moved slowly, the rhythm is slow, when it is fast they try to keep in time with the increased speed. Finally, when it is placed behind the person's back, everyone stops. Each person who wants to can become the magic conductor until the activity is finished.

Therapeutic purpose: Fun and very powerful way of building confidence as team members respond to the person holding the baton, teambuilding, enhancing self-esteem.

11
Contracts for change

A useful idea in the first session as a kind of ice-breaker with a new child or adolescent client is to introduce them to the sandtray or some small world objects and suggest the child shows in the sandtray or with the objects what it would look like when all the client's difficulties are solved.

After the child or young person has finished, the counsellor can ask what is going on with the objects, what it feels like, what is happening etc. It is best for the counsellor to keep in the third person (he, she, it, they) rather than using the word 'you', and in the present tense rather than the past or future. For the child/young person this positive psychology approach can have a beneficial effect in itself.

The ideas from this sandtray or small world creation can also form the basis of a mutually agreed *contract for change.* A contract in therapy has been defined as 'an explicit bilateral commitment to a well-defined course of action' (Stewart & Joines, 1987, page 328).The counsellor's part is to support the client in achieving the positive outcome the child/adolescent has shown in the sandtray or small world.

Therapists trained in person-centred and similar approaches may not be used to contracting with clients. Transactional analysis is a contract-based therapy in which clear goals are set in a positive way. According to Ian Stewart (1996), contracts are:

Positive – *What you want, not what you don't want.*
Sensory-based – *The result can be seen or heard.*
Finishable – *If, for instance, you want to be more friendly, how many friends will you need to make?*

The above approach can be used to help develop a treatment contract with a child in therapy.

Multiple contracts

One of the biggest differences for counsellors between working therapeutically with adults and therapy with children and young teenagers is the type of contract that is made. In UK law a child under 16 on their own can't make a contract. It's true that children often need bringing to therapy, and they usually need the agreement of their parents or guardians and payment by someone else. However, quite often even small children have an idea of how they want to be different as a result of therapy. They just have trouble putting it into words, yet they can often express it through inanimate objects.

The difference is that, whether the therapist works with an individual child or young person, a group of children or a family unit, there are always others involved in the contract. With adults, the confidentiality contract is usually agreed unless the person is going to harm themselves or harm others. With children the contract for confidentiality includes everything except harm to self, harm to others or if *someone is harming them.*

Another difference is that with individual adults there are just two people. With every child or young teenager the therapist works with there are at least three people involved in the contract: therapist, client and parent/guardian or teacher.

Fanita English (1975) identified this concept in terms of a visiting lecturer to a college. The lecturer works with the students (their contract). Yet both the lecturer and the students are answerable to, and therefore have a contract with, what English called the 'great powers'. She described the result as a Three-Cornered Contract.

More recently, therapists have adapted this concept to working with children and young people, calling it *Three-Handed Contracts.* (For more on this see Tudor, 2007, chapter 7.) The three points of the triangle are usually: Client, therapist and parent/guardian.

In the case of a student at school or in an agency there may be more than three people involved. They might additionally include teacher, headteacher, social worker and the courts. The result is two or more triangles linked between therapist and client. The counsellor will need to be aware of the contractual element with each of these and seek to satisfy each one.

Here are some components to consider for the three-handed contract: If the counsellor charges for the therapy, the parent will need to agree to pay. Unless the child is already in their usual school or old enough to travel alone, the child will need to be brought to the therapy. Even more important, in English and Welsh law a parent has the right to know what is discussed with their child under the age of 16 (see above). One of the agreements the therapist may have with the parent is that what is talked about is confidential. Of course, the parent will need to agree something similar with the child or young person.

In practice, the other parties to the contract are usually willing to go along with the parent's and the child's wishes. It is important to be aware, though, that the more people involved in the contract the trickier it can be to please everyone.

12
Sensory

Introduction

Everyone knows that there are five senses:

- *Hearing.*
- *Seeing.*
- *Touch.*
- *Taste.*
- *Smell.*

These senses are useful in therapy. Psychotherapist Eric Berne believed that a good clinician should use all five senses in diagnosis, assessment and treatment planning. While most therapists are skilled at sight and hearing, the other three senses are less well used. Berne writes: 'Good odours and bad odours should be noted, and this may require the resurrection of a sense of smell which has been severely repressed by social training . . . The sense of taste has become even more unfashionable as a clinical instrument than the sense of smell, even for diagnosing diabetes, and in group treatment there is seldom an occasion to use it unless the patient offers the therapist a candy, which may turn out to be sour or bitter' (Berne, 1966/1994, page 65).

Occupational therapists (OTs) have identified seven additional senses that have relevance when working therapeutically with children:

- *Body position.*
- *Balance and movement.*
- *Oral movement.*

- *Movement planning.*
- *Major movement.*
- *Fine movement skills.*
- *Bilateral coordination.*

This section explores practical applications of some of these 12 senses using activities with children and young people. We have taken what OTs have found and developed it for use in therapeutic work with children. Below is a story familiar to some young children that can be useful as a discussion starter.

The princess and the pea

This is the story of *The Princess and the Pea,* by Hans Christian Anderson:

There was once a prince, and he wanted a princess, but she must be a real princess.

He travelled right around the world to find one, but there was always something wrong. There were plenty of princesses, but whether they were real princesses he had great difficulty in discovering; there was always something that was not quite right about them. So at last he had come home again, and he was very sad because he wanted a real princess so badly.

One evening there was a terrible storm; with thunder and lightning and the rain pouring down in torrents; indeed, it was a fearful night.

In the middle of the storm somebody knocked at the town gate, and the old king himself sent to open it.

It was a princess who stood outside, but she was in a terrible state from the rain and the storm. The water streamed out of her hair and her clothes; it ran in at the top of her shoes and out at the heel, but she said that she was a real princess.

'Well, we shall soon see if that is true,' thought the old queen, but she said nothing. She went into the bedroom,

took all the bedclothes off and laid a pea on the bedstead: then she took 20 mattresses and piled them on top of the pea, and then 20 feather beds on top of the mattresses. This was where the princess was to sleep that night.

In the morning they asked her how she slept.

'Oh terribly bad!' said the princess. 'I have hardly closed my eyes the whole night! Heaven knows what was in the bed. I seemed to be lying upon some hard thing, and my whole body is black and blue this morning. It is terrible!'

They saw at once that she must be a real princess when she had felt the pea through 20 mattresses and 20 feather beds. Nobody but a real princess could have such a delicate skin.

So the prince took her to be his wife, for now he was sure that he had found a real princess, and the pea was put into the museum, where it may still be seen if no one has stolen it.

Now this is a true story.

Seekers and avoiders

Children and young people who have a similar condition to the princess are called *sensory defensive* or *sensory avoiders.* The terms are interchangeable. Clients with this condition may be born with it or acquire it though trauma, especially sexual or physical abuse. Children and teenagers on the autistic spectrum are more likely than others to be sensory avoiders, though this isn't a hard and fast rule.

Researchers have found that children deprived in their early years of emotional and sensory contact sometimes become depressed and withdraw from physical contact in spite of loving adoptive parents or foster carers. This is often known as Reactive Attachment Disorder.

Other children need more and more stimulation. They like to swing around, spin around and repeatedly jump up in the air. Often they are seen as hyperactive when they may well be what are called *sensory seekers.*

In a way all human beings have sensory issues. Winnie Dunn (2007) writes:

We experience a sense of calm with sensory experiences, and get overwhelmed with other sensory experiences . . . People will have their own personal lists of what sensory experiences are calming or overwhelming. Some of us readily search for new input, while others withdraw from situations to reduce the amount of input available.

It is important when working with young clients to identify their sensory issues and seek to meet those issues during the therapy, working with the parents where this is useful. Some of the activities suggested in this section may be suitable for sensory seekers but unsuitable for sensory avoiders – and the other way round. Before trying these activities with children or young people it is important to make sure the counsellor knows their client!

A useful tip is to find times when the child client is most responsive, then use those times for communication between client and therapist. Counsellors are advised to leave enough time for the client to request more of an activity that the child enjoys.

*In addition to the 12-year-old client having difficulties with socialising and thinking in a way different from his peers, he had sensory issues. Similar to many people on the autistic spectrum, he was a **sensory avoider** in terms of vision. He avoided eye contact so much that for one session he lay face down on the floor, talking from that position so he didn't have to look at the therapist. For the whole of another session the boy and the therapist talked while throwing a small soft toy to each other, back and forth, the focus being on the throwing rather than making eye contact.*

*Another sensory issue for the client was smell, the sense most closely associated with memory. In this case he was a **sensory seeker**. In the first session the young client walked over, picked the therapist's arm up, put his nose near it and sniffed the therapist's arm. 'You smell just like my* *mum,' he said. Later the mother confirmed that she used the same bland moisturiser as the therapist.*

In the final session the client arrived for the session wearing an obvious but pleasant aftershave. Towards the end of the session, as part of his goodbye, he sat on the floor with his back to the counsellor's feet and asked for a gentle massage. The counsellor massaged his shoulders and scalp as they talked.

It was only after the client and his mother had left that the counsellor noticed the lingering smell. His hands smelled of aftershave, no doubt as a result of the client plastering aftershave over his hair and clothes as well as his face. The smell lingered all afternoon in the counselling room. It was as if this young client, a sensory seeker of smell, had left his scent as a gift to the counsellor and the counselling work, a memory of himself in the form of a pleasant aroma.

Sensory processing disorder

Counsellors may come across children or young people who have considerable difficulty with the senses. It could be that they have the condition known as *Sensory Processing Disorder.* This used to be called Sensory Integration Dysfunction but the label has changed. Some of these children and young teenagers are very uncoordinated and often carry the label *dyspraxia.* Others may not be labelled as such but may still have difficulties in the area of the senses.

Much of the material we have used in our own sensory work with children comes from two excellent books written by OT Carol Kranowitz, *Out of-Sync Child* (Penguin, 1998) and *Out-of-Sync Child has Fun* (Kranowitz, 2003/2006). She has pioneered a lot of fun activities for out-of-sync children (those challenged by sensory issues). They are widely used by OTs and yet there is a clear link between OT work and therapeutic work used by counsellors and therapists. She writes:

The child who avoids ordinary sensations or seeks excessive stimulation, whose body is uncooperative, whose behaviour is difficult and who doesn't 'fit in' is our out-of-sync child. He receives sensory information just like everybody else . . . But, unlike most people, the child may misinterpret or be unable to use that information effectively (Kranowitz, 2003/2006, page 5).

The following activities can be used to help both sensory seekers and sensory avoiders to deal with what is troubling them. In our experience as therapists this also helps them to start facing the underlying emotional issues they have.

Choosing a stone

This activity involves choosing a stone from a selection. It is intended to cover the sensory areas of *seeing* (by choosing and observing its colours), *fine motor skills* (exploring the parts of the stone) and *touch* (feeling the stone's shape, coldness and smooth or rough edges).

The therapist should have a selection of stones available and invite the client to choose one. (Be cautious about using this activity if the client is likely to throw the stone or use it in a way that is inappropriate.)

The client is invited step by step to look at the colours, shape and size of the stone. The therapist suggests that the client feel the stone carefully, allowing themselves to experience its texture, temperature, rough edges or smooth parts. If they want to, they can close their eyes and let the stone's properties 'speak' to them.

At the end of the activity the therapist asks the client to say what it was like for them to see, feel and explore with their hands the stone they chose.

Therapeutic purpose: Choosing the stone can help to develop the child's confidence. Because the child or young person gets to keep the stone it can be seen as a form of transitional object, helping the client to 'take away' significant steps in their process of therapy.

Discovering your balance

Discovering Your Balance is an activity that involves walking on a rope. It is possible to use a clothesline instead or even a ribbon.

The rope is laid across the room in a pattern such as a zigzag. Clients may like to make their own patterns with the rope. This will stimulate their imagination. If the counsellor is working with a group of children or young people, they can be divided into pairs, with one person wearing a blindfold and the other guiding their partner. This takes some courage but can help with building trust.

There are various ways of doing this activity. Children can balance on the rope itself, balancing like a tightrope walker. Or they can put a foot on each side of the rope, feeling the rope between their feet. For extra sensory stimulation they can do this in socks or even barefoot. If they succeed and have the confidence, they can try walking backwards on the rope.

Finally, if working with a group they can form two teams and walk the rope together, each team starting from a different end. When a child meets someone from the other end, they move past the other person without stepping off the rope.

After the activity, the therapist invites discussion about what it was like for the child/children.

Therapeutic purpose: An ideal activity for *bilateral coordination, motor planning, balance and movement,* and *posture.* It is also helpful for stimulation through the feet and toes, especially if the client takes off their shoes. This activity is good for clients who are uncoordinated or have dyspraxia as well as simply a fun activity and challenging experience.

Slide whistle exercise

Another activity involving the senses is called *Slide Whistle Exercise*. It is fun for younger children and emphasises the predictability they need in order to feel good about themselves. It is best to use a slide whistle if at all possible. If not, a whistle with notes on it, such as a recorder, will do. The idea is that the higher the note the higher they put up their hands or feet. They can do this while sitting on a chair or lying down.

When the sound goes up they gradually put their arms in the air. When the sound goes down they gradually put them down. If it happens quickly they move their hands up or down quickly. When they are lying on the floor they can do the same with their legs. When the note goes up, they put their legs in the air. When the note goes lower, they put their legs down. This becomes even more fun for them when the therapist leaves the children with their legs partly in the air.

Finally, they can try doing sit-ups to the up-and-down sound.

Slide Whistle Exercise is not as easy as it sounds, especially if they are watching. The slide whistle's 'arm' goes in to produce a higher note and out to produce a lower one, which is completely contrary to what is expected. Children need to listen carefully to the note rather than look at the slide whistle.

By varying the speed of the slide, clients increase or slow down their movements. This can help with children who are hyperactive.

Therapeutic purpose: This activity promotes concentration and cooperation as well as listening skills. It emphasises the importance of relating *hearing* to *major body movement.* It inevitably causes plenty of laughter, which is therapeutic in itself.

Chocolate awareness

Not surprisingly, one of the most popular activities with children, young people and even adults is called *Chocolate Awareness.* It involves tasting chocolate in a completely different way from usual.

When working with children it is essential to check with parents/carers for any allergies they might have. For instance, chocolate bars often contain milk and may have traces of nuts such as hazelnuts and almonds, and these could cause major problems to someone with an allergy. As a final check ask the child if they have a peanut or milk allergy. If a client is allergic to the ingredients in chocolate, fudge could be considered as an excellent substitute. Again, check that the fudge doesn't contain anything the child might have an allergy to.

If using chocolate, the therapist chooses two different flavoured bars. Ideally one has in it texture such as crunchy pieces of mint as this adds an extra dimension to the experience.

Here is a suggested form of words for the exercise. (Remember, the therapist can join in at the same time!)

Please take two pieces of the chocolate and keep them until we are ready. You might need to put them on a piece of paper to stop them melting.

OK, on the count of three put one half into your mouth, but don't chew. One – two – three. Close your eyes and focus on the taste. Be aware of the sweet taste emerging as the chocolate melts. Focus on the rich taste. What does it feel like in contact with your tongue, lips, cheek and teeth? Let your whole mouth be full with the sensation of the chocolate.

Now chew slowly and swallow it, staying aware of what it is like at the back of your throat.

Take a piece of the crunchy chocolate. Imagine you are a cat and lick it lightly. Notice the taste on your tongue. This time on the count of three put it in your mouth and immediately begin chewing slowly. One – two – three. Be aware of the texture – the softness of the chocolate, the hardness of the bits in the chocolate and the two separate tastes. Also notice the taste of the two combined. OK, you can swallow when you are ready.

Now that we have finished, let's break up the remaining chocolate so that we get a chance to eat it in a 'normal' way.

What was that taste experience like for you?

Therapeutic purpose: This activity combines *taste, smell* and *oral-motor senses.* It can be useful for resensitising as well as for contacting feelings and senses that have been dulled through emotional difficulties, abuse or trauma. It can also encourage slowing down to taste and feel food – useful in the case of someone with issues related to ADHD (hyperactivity).

Silent-movie workouts

The *Silent-Movie Workouts* activity requires a metronome, available from music shops, or a noisy clock (such as an old-fashioned alarm clock) – or an app making similar sounds. Failing all else, the therapist can clap a rhythm.

The metronome is set to about 60 beats a minute (the musical speed known in Italian as Andante). The counsellor then leads the child or children in some warm-ups ready to start.

Once everyone is warmed up the idea is to follow the therapist's actions, keeping in time with the metronome. The actions could be simple exercises and stretches or more advanced activities, depending on the age of the child/children. After a minute or so the leading is passed on to a child. This continues until everyone taking part has had a chance to take the lead.

As children get used to the rhythm and pattern they will probably be amused when they are reminded that their jerky movements are similar to those of the actors in a very old black-and-white silent movie.

The counsellor needs to be aware that this exercise, because of its highly repetitive nature, could cause injury. It is important to watch carefully to make sure no one is over-exerting themselves.

Therapeutic purpose: This activity involves *bilateral coordination, motor planning* and *major movement.* The consistent, regular movements correlate approximately with a person's heartbeat, so children will hopefully feel coordinated. Those on the autistic spectrum will enjoy the consistency while those with hyperactivity will hopefully learn to pattern their actions in time with the metronome, which can help to regulate their pace. This activity is also an enjoyable way to help with group formation.

Adventures in taste

Adventures in Taste is about tasting unusual or surprising food items. It is vital to make sure that all products used are free of peanut residue and other allergens or check that children and young people are free of difficulties with allergens and can tolerate most foods. The counsellor is advised to avoid extremely strong or obnoxious tastes. Some foods may need to be kept refrigerated until needed.

The therapist may consider joining in this tasting experience as this will help young clients to be more experimental. It is important to assure young clients that everything is edible and that nothing is likely to harm them, burn their mouths or make them ill.

There are lots of edible items that can be tried. The counsellor could try exploring at a deli counter to find unusual foods. A useful one that we have tried several times is popping candy. Here is how we would lead it.

Open your hand and I'll give you something edible.

OK, this is some sweet powder to try. Close your eyes and put it in your mouth. Be aware of the taste. Now concentrate on what's happening in your mouth.

Do you like what you have tasted, or hate it?
Would you try it again?
Finally, can you identify what you have tried?

Therapeutic purpose: This activity is mildly risk-taking and adventurous. It focuses on *taste, oral-motor* and *hearing.* It can help children and young people to take small risks and make decisions for themselves. Above all, it is lots of fun.

13
Recommended training

The contents of this book originally formed the basis of an eight-day course of training leading to a Post-Graduate Certificate in Counselling Children and Families. This book on its own, however, will not enable a counsellor to become a specialist in working with children. In addition it will need elements of training in order to achieve that goal, both before working with children and as a form of Continuing Professional Development. We recommend eight days of training at the beginning and up to five days a year on an ongoing basis.

So how can a counsellor select the best kind of training to help them become competent and skilful in working with children, young people and families? There are many one- and two-day courses to choose from that could help the counsellor become more competent in working with children. They are often publicised in counselling magazines and websites.

As a general principle it is best to consider courses where there is a reasonable balance of practical to theory. As counselling primary school age children is usually 80 per cent practical to 20 per cent theory, it is important to get enough of the practical side of the training.

Then, it is often useful to consider what counselling models the therapist favours and give them priority. In addition to our own models, we sought training outside them – and not necessarily working with children – that helped with our work: creative experiment in gestalt therapy; dealing with dangerous people; introduction to Solution-Focused Therapy; understanding therapy through dance; dramatherapy; and many others.

Attending components of training in play therapy can also be helpful. The Rocky Mountain Play Therapy Institute in Calgary, Canada, offers components in working with younger children. See http://rmpti.com/

Therapists attending training courses don't have to implement everything they learn on a particular course; it's a case of taking what is helpful and leaving behind what isn't.

Practical application of creative techniques can be increased by working with peer groups.

Here are just a few ideas for the kind of courses that could be helpful:

- *Psychodrama.*
- *Working with autism and sensory issues.*
- *Groupwork.*
- *Creative sandtray/sandplay.*
- *Family therapy.*
- *Therapeutic work in schools.*
- *Art in therapy.*
- *Music in therapy.*
- *Therapeutic/adventure work outdoors.*
- *Training in self-care.*

14
Movement

Introduction

In this section we are going to look at movement, including dance. Although many counsellors don't tend to use movement much with children, we are enthusiastic to see it used more in therapy.

The focus in therapy using movement is not on children's or adolescent's problems. It isn't a case of concentrating on their symptoms, sickness, tensions and anxieties or levels of function. Movement is about helping the person to express themselves, usually without words.

The client had used her training in dancing within several sessions to help her deal with some of her deep-rooted issues. Just as things were starting to improve for her, an elderly relative who meant a lot to her suddenly died. After missing a session because of the grief she felt, the client arrived with a coat that had belonged to her relative. She kept smelling it and then invited the therapist to do the same. The smell was of an elderly person's cosmetics and it evoked strong memories for the client.

As the session progressed, the counsellor suggested that the client might want to dance with the coat. Holding the coat as if it were her dancing partner the client went round and round the room, dancing a waltz and occasionally spinning around. As she did so she smiled and seemed to enjoy the movement and the memories.

By the end of the dance the client was exhausted and tearful. She had used dance to express some of her heart for the dear relative she had lost.

Body movement activity

What is known as 'dance movement therapy' is based on the principle that movement reflects a person's thinking and feeling. Emotional changes can occur when the therapist encourages exploring new movement patterns. The phrases used below are based on Rudolph von Laban's movement principles (see Laban, 1966, and Laban, 2011/1950).

The counsellor can encourage the child or young person to try some of these movements to understand what they look like and then say how each movement felt. If the counsellor is working with a group of children or young people, they can ask for a volunteer from among the young clients to show them the movement and then the rest of the group all follow them. Depending on the age of the child/children some of the words may need explaining.

- **Body in action** – *whole body, body parts, joints moving, surfaces in contact.*
- **Body shape** – *symmetry, asymmetry, wide/open, curved, twisted.*
- **Body flow** – *successive, simultaneous, bound, free, sustained, impulsive.*
- **Action in body** – *jumping, turning, twisting, gesturing, stillness.*
- **Action in space** – *rising, sinking, gathering, scattering, advancing, retreating.*
- **Dimensions of space** – *personal, high, middle, deep, up, down, in front, behind, to the left, to the right.*
- **Dynamics** – *direct pathways, indirect pathways.*
- **Time** – *fast, slow, rhythmic, arrhythmic.*
- **Phrasing** – *long, short, accented.*
- **Quality** – *mood.*
- **Relationships** – *solo, duo, group.*
- **Proximity** – *near, far.*
- **Contact** – *touch, weight bearing, supporting.*

Therapeutic purpose: Enjoying various body movements, exploring stuck points, assessment by the counsellor of areas that may need therapeutic work.

Truck wash

Truck Wash is an activity that works best with a group of children or young people. When preparing to do this activity, the therapist can either buy cheap cheerleader's pompoms or, better still, get the young clients to help make their own brushes for the truck wash.

Each home-made brush consists of a large (dustbin-size) plastic sack, preferably in blue or another attractive colour. A knot is tied at the closed end of the bag and then, using strong scissors, thin strips are cut from the end right up to the knot. This is best achieved by one person holding the end with the knot and another person cutting the strips.

When the cutting is complete, the layered strips are carefully separated and spread out to form a brush that looks something like a cheerleader's pompom. This can take some time and effort to achieve. In our experience children love creating their own pompoms.

The counsellor explains to the children or young people that a large truck going down a busy motorway or main road is likely to pick up plenty of dirt, dust and road slush. This all needs cleaning off regularly so that the truck looks good and doesn't start to deteriorate and get rusty. In a similar way, the stress of life leaves people feeling contaminated. *Truck Wash* can help to 'wash away' the stress, leaving the client refreshed and invigorated.

The counsellor suggests that in pairs the clients practice brushing each other with the brushes. It is important to ensure that clients brush each other gently. There is a great temptation for boys in particular to use the brushes as beaters, which can sting badly.

Once they have finished practicing, the clients form two lines facing into the middle and each person take it in turns to dance up and down the line while the rest of the group gently brush the 'truck' clean, from head (roof) to foot (underside) and back again several times. The counsellor can invite the youngsters to make sure every area of the truck is gently cleaned.

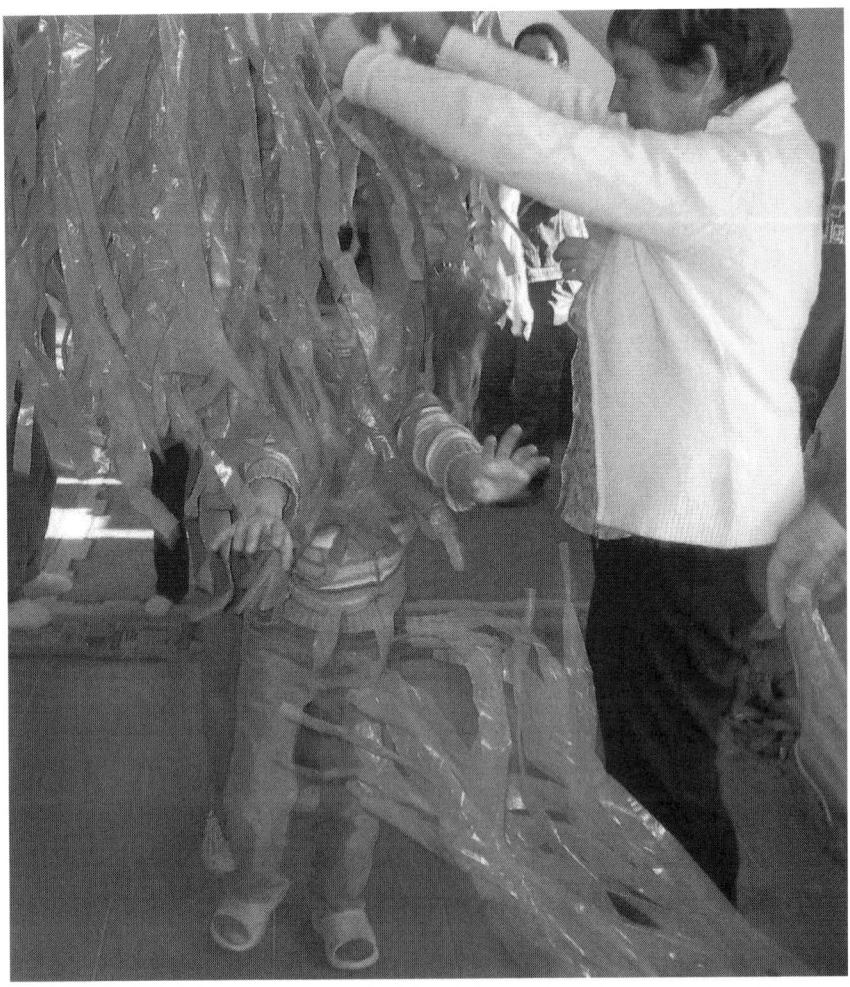

Any lively music can enhance this activity. We recommend the song *Car Wash,* by Christina Aguilera that featured in the film Shark Tale. Here is a link: https://www.youtube.com/watch?v=aVlpy5USN-E

Clients who have been abused as young children may at first find the swishing movements of the brushes a bit frightening but hopefully, if they can come through their initial reaction, they will soon enjoy safe contact with others. Be aware, though, that children and young people with serious sensory issues may find this activity difficult or even impossible.

Truck Wash is one of 64 activities about the body, including movement, in our book Body Awareness (Day & Day, 2008/2011).

Therapeutic purpose: This activity is highly effective for giving and receiving positive messages through gentle contact with the body. It is an excellent activity for building self-esteem and developing confidence.

Mirroring movement

Movement is a vital part of the process of therapy with children and young people. Sometimes the child simply moves in a rhythmic way. At other times they might move while playing a musical instrument or using a scarf or holding a toy such as an airplane.

When a young child begins to move in rhythm, it is very helpful if the therapist follows, mirroring approximately what the child is doing. By doing it approximately the therapist shows empathy with the child rather than cause annoyance by simply mimicking.

In the Mirroring Movement exercise the therapist observes carefully for an opportunity to begin the mirroring. They then begin following the client's movements. It is vital that the therapist checks nonverbally at each stage that the client is happy with what they are doing.

This exercise brings together keys skills in working therapeutically with children and young people. A counsellor working with adults has already learned about the place and importance of empathy. They will have learned about active listening and the tone of voice used. These are skills that can also apply to working with children. Three more skills used here are vital: *intuition, mirroring* and *nonverbal empathy.*

At the end of the *Mirroring Movement* it may be helpful for the counsellor to discuss with the child what it was like for their movement to be mirrored.

Therapeutic purpose: Confidence, self-esteem, focusing, acknowledgment and recognition.

Exploring the sea

For *Exploring the Sea* the idea is to gather together in advance pictures from magazines and other sources showing objects that are in and under the sea. The counsellor then explores them together with the child/children.

The client then decides to represent a type of sea creature. If the therapist is working with a group of children or young people, they can encourage two or three people to represent each different group of creatures. Some of the various creatures could be: crabs, swordfish, sea slugs, dolphins, sea anemones, seaweed, octopuses. Maybe there could be small fish to swim in and out of the coral reef.

Then it is time to practice the individual movements of the creature chosen. If dressing-up props are available they can enhance this activity.

Finally, the counsellor chooses some music to represent sea noises that can help to create an underwater scene. We prefer natural sea noises and have used the following track to good effect:

https://itunes.apple.com/us/album/underwater-cave/1031663375

Therapeutic purpose: Exploring the Sea encourages creativity and exploring of movement. It can be effective with most client groups including those with hyperactivity issues.

Ways of walking

Ways of Walking is an exercise to anchor good feelings by the way young clients move. The child, young people or group are invited to start walking around the room at their own pace and using their own pattern of walking.

Then they are asked to continue walking around the room in each the following ways:

- *Hopping.*
- *On tiptoes.*
- *As if string is attached to their fingers.*
- *As if string is attached to their nose.*
- *As if they've had a really good time.*
- *As if they're walking on the clouds.*
- *As if they're really happy.*
- *As if they've made some friends.*
- *As if they carry 100 balloons.*
- *As if the 100 balloons are carrying them.*
- *As if they are really proud of themselves.*

Once all these and similar *Ways of Walking* have been done, the counsellor initiates discussion about what it was like for the client/s. How did they feel after doing the activity?

Therapeutic purpose: Exploring movement and coordination, contacting feelings that may be repressed, having plenty of fun and laughter.

Rhythmic gymnastics

The next activity, *Rhythmic Gymnastics,* can be a beautiful and powerful way to express feelings. It will need two-metre lengths of coloured ribbon or special rhythmic gymnastics ribbons. The counsellor plays some gentle, expressive music of their (or their client's) choice. The client chooses the ribbon they want to use. They may find it more liberating to take off shoes and even socks for this activity.

As the music starts the client is invited to begin expressing themselves through their body, using the ribbon and while moving around the room. The therapist may decide to join in as well.

The freedom to express their feelings completely could be scary for clients and they may need to start very gently. During the activity the counsellor needs to watch carefully the client's face and body posture to see how they are coping and when they are ready to stop.

Afterwards, the therapist and the client discuss the activity in as much detail as the client wants and needs.

Therapeutic purpose: This activity will hopefully build the client's confidence and enable them to express through their bodies what they struggle to express in words. The freedom experienced by this activity may be seen as a metaphor for freedom from the difficulties they have faced in life that brought them to therapy in the first place.

Paper plate dance

The final exercise in this section, *Paper Plate Dance,* combines the three categories of Music, Movement and Sensory. The idea is to hit paper plates together in time with the music as if the plates were cymbals. Disposable plastic plates can be used, though the more gentle sound of paper on paper is best.

The plates are held vertically and banged together gently in time to the music. Different positions can be tried – behind the back, low down, high up, figure of eight.

If the therapist is working with an individual, then the two can perform together, taking it in turns to conduct the playing. If there is a group of young people, they each conduct with their paper plates before passing on the conducting to someone else. This can be done with a nod or by tapping gently on the shoulder.

When the music reaches a crescendo the conductor can make the *Paper Plate Dance* more dramatic, lifting the paper plates high up and using vibration as well as gentle banging. Everyone then follows in a similar way.

We have used music from Mozart, which has been shown to have a profound effect on people's creativity. His music has also been used in shopping centres where it has had a calming influence, discouraging violence and shoplifting. A suggested piece of music of Mozart that lasts about five and a half minutes is Eine Kleine Nactmusik Allegro:

https://youtu.be/FCi2u265wxQ

Therapeutic purpose: Team building, bilateral coordination, enjoyment, laughter.

15
Steps towards working with children

This section summarises steps for counsellors, currently working therapeutically with adults at Diploma level, to learn the skills and understand the theory needed to start working therapeutically with children, young people and families.

It is based on the requirements of our former Postgraduate Certificate in Therapy with Children and Families. The course aimed to give the basic tools needed for working with children and young people, including aspects of safety and safeguarding (child protection). Teaching included how to work with minors taking into account the needs and wishes of third parties involved with the child, such as parents/guardians, teachers and social workers.

The course sought to provide opportunities to practise techniques and creative approaches within the safety of the training room before attempting the same techniques in the therapy room with children.

The intention of the course was to provide an opportunity for people to become counsellors of children, young people and families as well as counsellors of adults so that counsellors and counselling organisations around the UK could open their doors to a new client group.

Here are the requirements of the course and the recommendations for counsellors seeking to become competent in working with children, young people and families:

Summary

The person is expected to have a Diploma in Counselling or equivalent and some experience in therapeutic work with adults.

Counsellors are strongly recommended to attend at least eight days (48 hours) of training in counselling skills with children, young people and families, including substantial personal experience of using the activities they plan to provide in therapy for young clients. They will also be expected to meet the following conditions:

■ Have in place an *Enhanced DBS Check* and be willing to keep this up to date with training in safeguarding skills (usually once every two years). (See chapter 3.)

■ Enter a *supervision arrangement* of their work with children, young people or families with a supervisor suitably qualified/experienced in therapy with children, young people or families or creative techniques. (See Introduction.)

■ Be *the lead therapist in a minimum of 30 sessions* with children, young people or families, while having frequent extra supervision.

■ Do an *infant/child observation* of play and communication over a minimum of six weeks and write up the results, submitting it to their supervisor for assessment. (See chapter 7.)

■ Write a *case study* of around 3000 words about a child they have worked with and submit the study for assessment by their specialist supervisor. The case study is intended to show the therapist's journey with their client – child, young person, group or family – over at least six weeks. The case study involves looking at the presenting issues, family dynamics and any other outside stresses. It continues with an idea of how the child wants to change. It then moves on to explore what is done and talked about in the sessions, with details of how the child uses creativity and significant points reached during the therapeutic process. The important thing is also to include the therapist's own journey in the therapeutic process, any difficulties they encountered – and how they resolved them.

■ Write an *essay* of approximately 3000 words about an aspect of their work with children, young people or families or an area of therapy with this age group they are interested in. The counsellor might want to write about a client group or children/young people with a particular difficulty. They could explore in depth how they might work with particular kinds of child or adolescent clients, such as those with autistic spectrum difficulty or ADHD, or children or young people with sight impairment. There is lots of flexibility for creativity. This too needs submitting for assessment by their specialist supervisor.

■ Write a *diary* about the counsellor's own process during preparation for working with children, while they are engaged in training, therapy with children and related supervision. Please note that this is about the counsellor's internal process and not about the content of the training undertaken or therapy/supervision sessions.

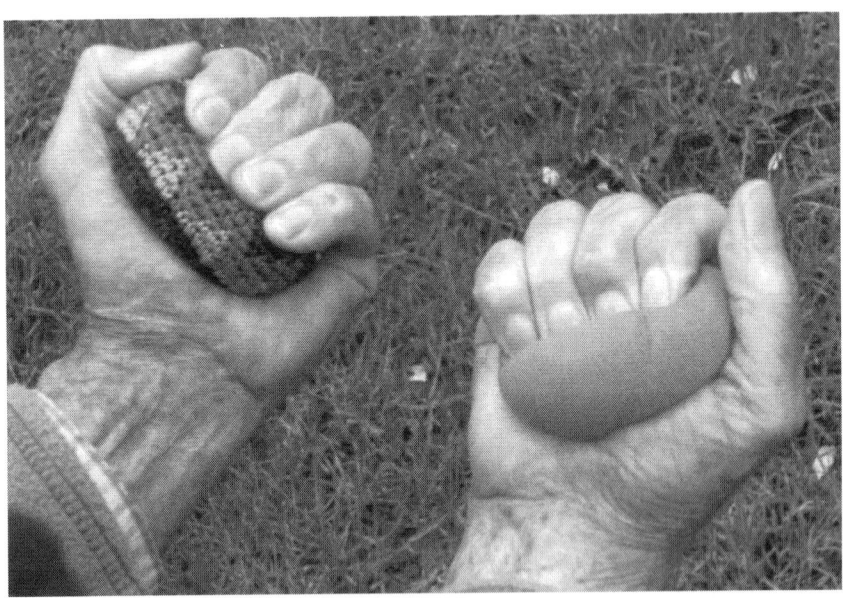

16
Emotions

Introduction

When a person – child, young person or adult – reaches the stage of needing to see a counsellor, they are often described as having an *emotional* difficulty. Children in particular are highly emotional beings and when something goes wrong it is often displayed in the area of the emotions.

According to the Transactional Analysis psychotherapy model there are four true (authentic) feelings or primary emotions (English, 1971):

- *Sad*
- *Happy*
- *Angry*
- *Scared*

This section explores these primary emotions because they are so important to children's and young people's healthy development. (Of course, there are numerous subdivisions within those primary emotions.) Also in this section is an explanation of true feelings that are covered up and show themselves as quite negative 'racket' feelings. Finally, the importance of emotional literacy is explored, with ways to help children and young people become emotionally literate.

We start with the primary emotions: Sad, Happy, Angry, Scared. A well-adjusted child or young person will have a good mixture of all four. A client can be sad about losing something or someone. They can be happy just for the sheer joy of it. They can be angry in a healthy, constructive way. And they can experience appropriate scare when, for instance, they look first before crossing the road or face a new situation.

Adults coming to therapy generally talk and think about their difficulties. Children, on the other hand, focus on their feelings and usually express them through play. Teenagers may prefer a mixture of both. Feelings are as important to a child as thinking is to an adult. It makes sense in therapy with children, therefore, to start working with feelings as early in the therapy as possible.

The young client was part of a therapy group centred on anger issues. Although in the group she tended to melt into the background, she took part quietly in all the activities. When it came to her turn to use the inflatable punchbag, however, she suddenly came to life. The counsellor had explained to the group that they could express their bad feelings, particularly anger, by punching, kicking or banging the punchbag hard. That way they could get rid of those unhelpful feelings without hurting themselves or other people or damaging property. This particular client, although the smallest child in the group, punched, elbowed and kicked furiously with shoes off until – sweating at the end – she stepped away smiling. Although the therapist would probably never know what caused the girl's fury, it was clear that she had dealt with her feelings in a safe, appropriate way.

Emotion corners

This activity is known as *Emotion Corners*. It can be used with an individual child/young person or as a group exercise. (It is very effective with adults, too.)

The counsellor sets up the room by writing one of the words Happy, Sad, Angry, Scared on each of four pieces of paper. The words are placed in the four corners of the therapy room together with several sheets of paper and felt pens. Alongside each emotion sheet a list is placed with the following questions:

- **How** do you feel when you have this emotion?
- **Where** in your body do you feel it?
- **How** do you show it on your face?
- **What** do you want to do when you feel like this?
- **What** colour comes to your mind as you think about that feeling?

The therapist then invites the client/s to walk around the room slowly and when they get to a corner that inspires them think about that emotion. They then read the questions and consider the answers for themselves. If children are not yet able to read, the phrases can be read out in advance.

Once the young person has gone to all four corners they are invited to sit down and discuss with the counsellor their answers to some or all of the questions.

Then they go around to all the corners again. This time they stop and draw a picture or some pictures of the emotion on a piece of paper. Or, if they want to, they can write things down. They could write the answer to the questions or words that are significant for them with this emotion. They might write prose or a poem to express that feeling.

When the exercise is finished the counsellor and client/s look together at the pictures and anything written down and the client tells the counsellor (and if appropriate the group) about what they have drawn or written – if they want to.

Therapeutic purpose: Exploring emotions in depth and perhaps identifying one or more that the client finds difficult to express.

Real and cover-up feelings

In the next few sections there are some more activities about feelings. First, though, we will look at what are known as *racket feelings* or *cover-up feelings.* The word *racket* comes from an American term, especially during the Great Depression of the 1930s, when gangsters in Chicago would sell illegal alcohol during prohibition and engage in illegal ways of making money. Usually the illegal activity was *covered up* while legitimate trade was apparently going on.

In most families one or more of the primary emotions is not allowed to be shown. It is usually an unspoken rule. For instance, in many British families anger isn't allowed but rather is *covered up* by other feelings. However people may feel, they often say when asked: 'I'm fine, thanks.' Japanese families generally don't show sadness.

When a person feels anger, it is often *covered up* by another feeling. Racket feelings are ways we all learn to manipulate those around us to get what we want without expressing the feeling in an authentic way.

Racket feelings can include embarrassment, jealousy, guilt, shame, depression or vague terms such as lost, stuck, cornered, helpless, desperate. (For more on this see Stewart & Joines, 1987, pages 166, 212-3.)

In his book for young children, *Being Mad Being Glad,* Roger wrote about racket feelings: 'We have cover-up feelings, such as *jealousy* and *loneliness,* so we do not have to show or deal with how we really feel. Cover-up feelings leave us feeling bad or *confused* . . . It is best to show your real feelings so people can understand you and help you. It you can't, talk to somebody' (Day, 2004, page 5).

Feelings tree

On page 140 there is a picture of the *Feelings Tree* with its little jelly-like characters in various positions in relation to the tree. This is a useful tool for assessing clients' emotional state. This is copyright free to photocopy for clients to use.

The idea is for the child or young person to put a circle around the person or colour them to show that is what they are like right now. Explain to young children that they do this without doing too much thinking. For older children the instruction could be: 'Use your intuition to circle or colour in the person that is most like you right now.'

Afterwards the counsellor asks the question: 'How do you feel about showing me the person you are now?' or

'What does it feel like to acknowledge your emotional state in this way?'

If working with a group the counsellor could say: 'Discuss with a partner where on the tree you feel you are and what that's like for you right now.'

Therapeutic purpose: Assessment, self-awareness, clinical governance.

Photographic feelings

Although *Photographic Feelings* is designed as a group activity, it can be adapted for use with an individual client or a family as well as a group.

Almost every situation involves more than one feeling. For instance, a bereavement usually includes stages of denial, anger, sadness, joy at good memories, new normality and moving on. It is important for children and young people to recognise this change in emotions in order to ask for what they need at each stage.

The group divides into smaller teams, depending on the number of clients in the group. Each team then thinks of a theme for a dramatic story with plenty of emotion in it. Examples might be: a huge fire, being attacked by a lion or watching a soccer match.

The teams are instructed to work out the story, then show it using everyone in their team as three photographs of feelings: the beginning, the climax and afterwards. On page 142 there is a list of feeling words grouped into the four primary emotions. The teams each choose three words to illustrate their story.

Once the children or young people have practiced in their small team, the group come back together and each team performs for the rest of the group.

Therapeutic purpose: Looking in depth at feelings and how they are expressed. Contacting feelings that might have been suppressed.

Grief and loss

One of the important areas of working with children or young people is helping them with grief and loss. If they have lost a person in death, or they have lost a friendship or a familiar place (moving house or school, for example), they are likely to go through a cycle of grief.

Feeling words

Sad
Bored
Sleepy
Inferior
Inadequate
Miserable
Depressed
Stupid
Ashamed
Guilty
Bashful

Happy
Peaceful
Relaxed
Loving
Trusting
Thankful
Hopeful
Excited
Playful
Creative
Cheerful

Angry
Jealous
Hurt
Selfish
Frustrated
Irritated
Critical
Hateful
Rage
Furious
Hostile

Scared
Anxious
Embarrassed
Rejected
Discouraged
Confused
Helpless
Insecure
Bewildered
Insignificant
Submissive

Adrienne Lee (1996) has identified a series of what she has called normal grief manifestations, including:

- *Shock.*
- *Sadness.*
- *Anger.*
- *Guilt.*
- *Anxiety.*
- *Helplessness.*
- *Confusion.*
- *Restlessness.*

To these we would add:

- *New normality,* and the final stage:
- *Moving On.*

As the child or adolescent works through the stages of grief it is important that they are provided with help and support. First they need permission to play, laugh and enjoy as well as to express what could be seen as the more negative emotions. Then they need help to validate the loss and make as much sense of it as is possible.

If the therapist is working with others in exploring ways to work with children therapeutically, it might be useful to imagine together having a child client or a family who has lost someone in death. Then plan a series of creative activities that will help the child/family to express the grief at the different stages.

Here are some ideas for a child, young person or family grieving:

- *Picture to say goodbye.*
- *Helium balloon or paper lantern with label to write message.*
- *Planning to plant a tree or rose.*
- *Candles, candle holders.*
- *Pebble painting.*

- *Create a mosaic.*
- *Dolls' house showing life then and life now.*
- *Write a song.*
- *Photo collage.*
- *Put flowers in oasis.*
- *Paper chains.*
- *Helium balloon with seeds inside.*
- *Memory box.*
- *Chalk colours.*
- *Bookmarks.*
- *Clay figures.*
- *Write letters.*

Therapeutic purpose: Enabling a young client to express in a visual, concrete way appropriate feelings for a loss in their life.

Happy tears, sad tears

The exercise *Happy Tears, Sad Tears* was originally designed for use in groups. It can also be used in families and with individual children and young people. The counsellor sources and then produces two small, clear semiprecious stones. Two glass beads of different colours could also be used. The counsellor describes them as ways of helping the group to remember their happy tears and their sad tears.

Here is a suggested way of explaining them:

This one is happy tears. As we pass it round tell the group of a time when you laughed so hard that tears came to your eyes. No comments or discussion by anyone other than the person holding the happy tear.

Then:

This one is sad tears. As we pass it round tell the rest of us about a time when you were so sad that tears came to your eyes. Again, no comments by others.

If it seems appropriate, the counsellor can ask for comments after everyone has finished. In our experience, though, this exercise often leads to a lot of emotion and it is useful to have a break or go on to a more light-hearted activity afterwards.

Therapeutic purpose: Exploring for some young clients the delicate subject of sadness and giving permission to express it in a safe, appropriate way.

Volcano

Volcano is an exercise related to *fear* needing five volunteers so it's really for groupwork only. One volunteer crouches down and the other four make a volcano by bringing their hands together over the person. The client crouching down then breaks out of the volcano with lots of noise and cheers and is then free.

The idea of this is to help young clients face scares and know they are safe and can break out of the imagined volcano in their lives. *It is absolutely important to ensure that the client has already done some group or individual therapy and that the counsellor is sure they will not be traumatised by this activity.* Also, ensure that the four clients standing up keep their heads out of the way and for safety don't wear glasses or pendants during the exercise.

Sometimes a fear can be overcome using *Volcano*. One time we used it with a child who had a fear of barking dogs. When he was about to break through the volcano we all barked like dogs and he broke free!

Some clients will want to do this activity several times until they are ready to move on.

Therapeutic purpose: A group activity to encourage young clients to face up to their fears in a fun yet safe way. Can promote trust and confidence.

Anger expression

In his book *Being Made Being Glad* Roger (see Day, 2004, page 6) has defined anger for young children as follows:

*Anger is a release of **energy** that can help you sort out your problems or protect you from harm. You get angry when someone is hurting you or if something doesn't seem right or fair. When you are angry you can also get sulky or stroppy. You may want to damage things or hit people.*

Your anger affects other people, so find a safe way to let it out:

- *Write it down or draw it.*
- *Count to ten.*
- *Shout loudly.*
- *Kick a ball or run fast.*
- *Punch a pillow.*
- *Tear up unwanted paper.*

It is important for young clients to know that safe expression of anger is healthy and normal and that repression of anger leads to physical and emotional problems. Rather than *anger management* we recommend *anger expression and violence management.*

In our book *Creative Anger Expression* (Day & Day, 2012b) we give lots of practical ideas for expressing anger safely within the therapy room. It is vital always that children, young people or families agree to safety rules before starting anger expression. These are:

- *Respect yourself.*
- *Respect the therapist.*
- *Respect things around you.*

Therapeutic purpose: Appropriate anger expression in a safe, contained environment.

Tearing paper

Probably the easiest form of anger expression and violence management is *Tearing Paper.* It is important to tell young clients that not all paper can be torn up so they don't destroy valuable paper items at home or school. Counsellors can save up unwanted takeaway menus and junk mail for anger expression.

Each person is invited to take a handful of junk mail. The counsellor explains (and demonstrates) that there are two ways of ripping paper. One is to tear it gently between thumb and forefinger. This does nothing for anger expression. The other way is to rip it suddenly and with force, possibly making a noise with the mouth. This is highly effective for anger expression.

The children or young people tear the paper together, tearing it into tiny pieces and being encouraged to put force into the tearing.

A fun part of the exercise for child and teenage clients is to throw the little pieces into the air. There is often lots of laughter and relief in doing this.

Once it is done, the young clients are invited to gather up all the pieces and throw them with some force into a bin. Then the therapist removes the bin from the room, symbolically removing the anger that has been expressed.

Once the *Tearing Paper* exercise is completed the counsellor invites discussion and comments about it.

Therapeutic purpose: Team work, helping young clients to become confident in themselves, knowing themselves, expressing anger safely and appropriately.

Stress ball

Another very effective way of expressing anger and managing violence is for children, young people and families to use a *Stress Ball.* Stress balls come in various sizes and shapes and it is useful to have several available in the counselling room. It is good practice to give young clients a stress ball and explain that it can be used for regular anger expression and people won't think it is weird to have a ball lying around in their bedroom.

It is useful to give a word of warning to children and young people that if they twist the stress ball in two hands it will probably break and be no longer any good for anger expression.

Invite the client to take a stress ball and hold it in *one* hand. The best way to do this is to hold it at arm's length and squeeze hard until the muscles in their arms start to shake. Making a noise with their mouth can help. Then they release the stress ball, relax their muscles and start to feel calm.

Discussion afterwards is useful.

Therapeutic purpose: Experience has shown that a stress ball used properly and regularly, even when the child or teenager isn't particularly angry, can be an important way for the child client to release anger and manage any violent outbursts.

Emotional literacy

One of the strongest advocates for emotional literacy was the late radical psychiatrist Dr Claude Steiner (1935-2017). He defined it on his former website as 'a heart-centred practice of emotional intelligence which results in an improvement in interpersonal relations and cooperation as well as personal well-being and success'. He also wrote: 'Being emotionally literate means that you know how to manage your emotions because you understand them' (Steiner, 2003, page 23).

'To be emotionally literate,' he wrote, 'is to be able to handle emotions in a way that improves your personal power and improves the quality of life around you. Emotional literacy improves relationships, creates loving possibilities between people, makes cooperative work possible, and facilitates the feeling of community' (Steiner, 1999, page 11).

*The therapist remembers when he was 11 and ready to leave his primary school. His teacher made it a very special event, giving the children time to realise and come to terms with the loss. The class had a party. The teacher said that the children could call him by his name, not Sir, if they were to see him in the street. They had a class picture taken and the young boy looked round and saw all the girls with wet stuff in their eyes. He and the other boys had prickly eyes and kept rubbing them. It was a moment in time that he has always remembered. It was the therapist's very first experience of **emotional literacy.**

Clear communication

Most people remember Einstein's formula: $E = MC^2$. We propose a new formula for working therapeutically with children and young people:

*Emotional literacy = **M**y understanding of feelings multiplied by many **C**onvincing responses (from teachers, parents and others) **S**quared*

In this context **S**quared hopefully means multiplied many times over. As children and young people develop a better understanding of their emotions and start to understand and practice emotional literacy, other people will respond in a positive way that will further build up their emotional resources.

There are six steps to emotional literacy:

1 Clear communication.
2 Positive affirmations.
3 Nonjudgmental statements.
4 Understanding assumptions about emotions.
5 Asking for what the person wants.
6 Apologising when it is needed.

Thinking about clear communication, Malcolm Gladwell (2005) describes how researchers Paul Ekman and Wallace Friesen spent a lifetime developing a system for understanding the 3000 different facial expressions that communicate something. Interestingly, Ekman points out that the information on our face is not just a signal of what is going on inside our mind. In a sense, it *is* what is going on inside our mind. When he uses his techniques to make an expression of anger, he says, 'My heartbeat will go up ten to 12 beats. My hands will get hot. As I do it, I can't disconnect from the system. It's very unpleasant, very unpleasant.'

Feeling faces

On page 152 there is a sheet of cartoon faces, all making different emotional expressions. For the *Feeling Faces* activities the therapist can copy this sheet or research another one to fit with specific clients.

In order to help a child become emotionally literate it is often useful to play games with these kinds of faces. Rather than this book giving all the answers, counsellors can use the faces that show emotions to work out one or more emotional literacy game they can use in their work with clients.

Ideas include:

- *Snap.*
- *Pairs.*
- *Bingo.*
- *Who would you take and why?*
- *Group the faces.*
- *Use the faces to tell a story.*
- *Stick pictures of the different faces on hardboiled eggs.*
- *Make finger puppets with feelings faces.*
- *Game of opposites.*
- *Role play.*
- *Card game.*

When working with a group, counsellors could divide the group into two teams. Each team then devises a game that they introduce to or play with the other team.

Therapeutic purpose: A useful way of developing emotional literacy, young clients knowing themselves and learning to be comfortable in their own skin.

Alien visitors

Alien Visitors is an exercise that can be done with an individual client or in group therapy with children, young people and families.

The idea is for the client/s to imagine they are aliens who have newly arrived on the earth. They then think of various emotions and describe what they as aliens would see. What shape is the mouth when a particular emotion is being shown? Are the eyes wide or narrowed? Is the forehead creased or relaxed?

Rather than notice the emotion by internal feelings, they do their best to describe the emotion in purely mechanical ways: The mouth is turned up at each corner, the eyes are wide open, etc. A useful way to do this is to look at various pictures cut out of magazines that show different emotions. They then study each picture and see what physical characteristics are shown by certain emotions.

Therapeutic purpose: Alien visitors is a great activity for children and young people on the autistic spectrum and others with 'face blindness'. It is also useful for all young clients to help them to know and understand what feelings are associated with a particular facial expression. By understanding feelings better in this way they are increasing their emotional literacy.

Positive affirmations

In addition to emotions, *Positive Affirmations* are a vital part of emotional literacy. Many counsellors working with children and young people are taught to avoid positive affirmations in therapy. We take a different view. It is important to avoid making positive comments on what a client creates on paper or in the sand, because the creation may be something very negative that the child or young person is working through. However, positive affirmations in our view can be made about children themselves and about positive changes in their lives that they report.

On the subject of positive affirmations, psychiatrist Dr Eric Berne introduced the concept of drives or hungers that are common to all human beings (Berne, 1970). Three of those he identified were:

■ *Stimulus/sensation hunger – examples include the thrill of roller coasters and the need for prisoners to avoid solitary confinement at all costs.*
■ *Recognition hunger – the need for someone to acknowledge them.*
■ *Structure hunger – the importance, for instance, of groups and organisations.*

Tony White later added another hunger:

■ *Attachment hunger, a biological, psychological and social hunger for an attachment to a caretaking figure.*

In his article he writes: 'This hunger persists throughout our lives. However, from adolescence onward, peer attachments allow the childhood need for a parental attachment to decrease . . . *without at least one firm and secure attachment in adulthood there is also mental and physical decline*' (White, 1997, italics added).

Of these four hungers, the main focus in this book is on stimulus/sensation hunger and recognition hunger. Babies need more than just milk. They need the sound, smell, warmth and touch of a significant other person, usually a mother. In other words, they need *recognition* from someone else. As a child grows, the child continues to need that recognition.

Berne introduced an unusual word – 'stroke' – to describe what the child needs. 'Stroke' can mean a blood clot on the brain or, in the past, a child being hit for being naughty. Berne used the word stroke to describe the action a mother naturally does with her newborn baby – stroking the back of their head. Berne called the stroke a 'unit of recognition' (Berne, 1970). Others describe it as 'the fundamental unit of social action'.

As babies grow, they continue to need strokes – physical and verbal. In fact, research has shown that without any strokes a baby will just give up and die. Researcher Dr Rene Spitz discovered in the 1940s that babies who were denied physical contact suffered a shrivelling up of the spinal cord called marasmus. In orphanages studied by Spitz and his colleagues, over a third of the babies died from 'broken hearts', despite being well fed and receiving good medical attention.

The term marasmus has in more recent decades come to refer to any severely malnourished child. However, many of the children who were institutionalised in Romania after the 1989 Revolution suffered incredibly because of the complete lack of physical contact or acknowledgement from the totally untrained staff. Many of those, too, died not from lack of food but purely from lack of stimulation. This was the form of marasmus Dr Spitz originally wrote about.

Fifteen or so years later, just before we moved to live in Romania for four years, we visited the unmarked abandoned children's corridor in a Romanian hospital. There we met small children unloved by parents as well as hospital staff. Sick babies were tied into their cots and all babies were rationed to two nappy changes a day. Nurses were adding extra water to the formula milk, leading to malnourishment.

Only charity workers and visitors such as us made any form of physical contact with these little ones. We stroked the face of a young girl with severe cleft palette and Roger held with great difficulty a two-year-old boy with a head larger than a football because of untreated hydrocephalus. We were witnessing extreme neglect that could well lead to marasmus.

The young woman in the UK told the counsellor her story: 'I was woken up in hospital on the night after giving birth and told that my baby girl was dying. At the special care unit I asked if I could hold my dying baby one last time. Cuddling my tiny infant I instinctively stroked the back of my baby's head. I spent the rest of the night cuddling my little one and stroking her head. For many days I continued doing this until, to my delight and the amazement of the doctors and nurses, my baby turned the corner and started to thrive. Four years later the medical staff were still talking about me, the mother who cuddled her baby back to life!'

Ideally, children need positive strokes on a regular basis. In fact, researchers have discovered that a child needs on average one positive stroke every 20 minutes throughout the day to grow up healthy emotionally.

Many children and young people don't get enough positive strokes so they start asking for negative ones instead. They might scream loudly so they get told off. They might hit a little brother or sister so they get into trouble with a parent. They might do badly in an exam so their teacher gets angry.

For the child or adolescent, any stroke is better than no stroke at all.

There are four different kinds of stroke:

- *Negative conditional.*
- *Negative unconditional.*
- *Positive conditional.*
- *Positive unconditional.*

Negative conditional
Negative conditional strokes are based on the child's behaviour. An example might be: 'You're always fighting with James', or: 'Don't let David near the paints. He causes trouble.' If the therapist is working with children, get them to think of some other negative conditional strokes that they may have heard.

Negative unconditional
The worst possible strokes are negative unconditional. If a parent consistently says to a child or young person: 'I wish you'd never been born', there is no way out for the child. A young person just can't help being born. Again, clients may well be able to think of other negative unconditional strokes.

Positive conditional
Positive conditional strokes are very popular, especially at school. Phrases such as 'Well done!' for something a child or young person achieves are often used. These kinds of strokes are usually given for things that the child or teenager does or what they wear. Children and young people will probably be good at listing other forms of positive conditional strokes.

Positive unconditional
Positive unconditional strokes are the very best strokes a child, young person or adult can have. They are strokes for being: 'I love you', 'You're special', 'I'm glad you were born,' 'I enjoy being with you.'

Therapists could talk about each child, young person or family group they work with and, possibly in supervision, come up with a positive unconditional stroke that is appropriate for using the next time they see that particular individual.

It is important to recognise and accept for the time being that some children and especially teenagers may refuse both positive unconditional strokes and any other strokes they are offered. Stewart & Joines (1987) write: 'Persons who have had a specially painful childhood may decide it is unsafe to let in any strokes at all. These people keep up a stroke filter so tight that they turn aside virtually all the strokes they are offered' (page 77).

For more details on different kinds of stroke and their effect on people read Stewart & Joines, 1987, pages 72-86.

Stroke messages

A counsellor working with children and young people can provide the impetus for clients to create stroke messages for their friends and, if appropriate, their families. After explaining to the client about positive strokes, conditional and unconditional, the client can create attractive cards with *Stroke Messages* (written or drawn, depending on their age and ability) to give to individuals outside the therapy room.

Normally materials such as artwork produced in the therapy room stay with the counsellor until the course of therapy is completed. In this case the stroke messages can become part of the client's own therapeutic journey. In most cases, children and young people will tend to write or draw strokes for others that they need for themselves. This then becomes a way for clients to understand the strokes they themselves need.

Therapeutic purpose: Confidence building, appreciating qualities in other people, empathy.

Marbles as strokes

Marbles as Strokes is an excellent activity when working with a children's therapy group that has already had a few sessions so that the children know each other well. (It has worked well with adult groups, too.) It is a game to help practice giving positive strokes.

The counsellor invites the children in the group to give positive strokes to each other. Children are told that these need to be genuine strokes. Each child then takes a handful of marbles. The idea is for each person to give their marbles away, one at a time, by saying something positive or giving an appropriate physical stroke (such as a handshake, high-five or hand on shoulder) to someone else in the group.

The challenge is that one person in the group ends up with less marbles than anyone else by the time the activity finishes. Usually, most children taking part seem to have a similar number of marbles at the end.

Therapeutic purpose: The activity *Marbles as Strokes* is fun and causes plenty of laughter. It also helps to emphasise the importance of giving and receiving positive strokes.

You're welcome

Many children and teenagers who come to therapy will have low self-esteem. Some deep down will feel 'left out' and 'not wanted'. *You're Welcome* is a powerful activity that can help children and young people feel more accepted and wanted. It is based on the ultimate unconditional positive stroke of *acceptance.* We are grateful to Jean Illsley Clarke for the practical ideas she demonstrated at various workshops that we are using for this activity.

In her book *Self-Esteem: A family affair* Jean Illsley-Clarke (1998/1978) identifies what she calls 'affirmations for being – deciding to live'. These are intended primarily for parents to use with their own children, though many of them can also be used in therapy. Here are the relevant ones:

- *I am glad you are alive.*
- *You belong here.*
- *What you need is important to me.*
- *I am glad you are you.*
- *You can grow at your own pace.*
- *You can feel all your feelings.*
- *I love you and I care for you willingly.*

In a therapeutic setting the last one could be adapted to something like:

■ *I appreciate you and I support you willingly.*

The therapist explains to the child or teenage client about feeling welcomed. Then they look together through the list of affirmations for being. When the client spots one or more of these that they don't identify with at the moment, the counsellor asks how they would like to be welcomed into the therapy group using those words.

Ideas might include the counsellor celebrating, clapping or cheering the client as she walks into the room or from the other side of the room. It might involve balloons or bubbles. Whatever the client wants, within reason, will help them to feel welcome deep down.

If the therapist is working with a group, two people stand in the middle and hold hands or each put a hand on the other's shoulder. Then they invite individuals one by one to come and join them and link together in the middle until everyone is linked in the middle.

Then the therapist talks about acceptance and feeling welcomed and invites anyone who wants to experience being welcomed to stand away from the group. Each person in turn is asked how they want to be welcomed by the group. It could be a tunnel of appreciation similar to the way football and rugby players form after friendly matches. It could be with hugs, cheers, clapping or some other way of greeting.

In our experience, once the first volunteers in the group have been welcomed, other group members will want to experience something similar. It is important that everyone who wants to experience acceptance is allowed to take part. It is also OK if some group members decide that this isn't for them.

Asking how people feel at the end of this activity may not be necessary because it frequently results in both tears and laughter and has a lasting impact on the clients.

Therapeutic purpose: Powerful acceptance, particularly for young clients who have felt left out, appreciation of self, teamwork.

17
Learning outcomes and objectives

Although this book in itself does not represent a training course, it is still important for the counsellor wanting to work with children or young people to have learning outcomes and objectives.

The suggested learning outcomes relate to what counsellors are expected to learn and achieve by the end of their preparation. Using the model developed by the University of Warwick (2017), the skills and knowledge a participant will possess upon successful completion of their preparation and training cover:

1. Subject knowledge and understanding

The participant will have a basic understanding of the difference between therapy with children, young people and families and therapy with adults. They will understand some of the theory behind a child learning through play and how that theory can be related to the therapy room. Through actual infant/child observation the participant will understand how creative therapy can help child and adolescent clients to achieve their developmental potential and reduce the negative effects of early trauma.

2. Subject-specific skills

Through peer and supervision work the counsellor will learn a wide range of creative techniques for working in therapy with children and families. Group activities with other counsellors will expand the counsellor's skills, especially in doing therapy with groups of children or with larger families. Skills will be honed through actual therapy with child clients (30 sessions), with extra specialist supervision.

3. Cognitive skills

Counsellors will develop new ways of understanding and assessing the effectiveness of therapy with children, young people and families by developing skills in intuition, metaphor and simile. They will learn to trust the process, without interpretation, while with the child or young people and then to use their cognitive skills in analysing the work for themselves and for their supervision.

4. Key skills

Counsellors will have added to their previous training and practice important skills in understanding and working with children, young people and families that can be transferred to therapy with children and families in agencies and in private practice.

18
Specific difficulties

Every therapist working with young clients will from time to time come across those who don't seem to fit into the usual pattern of therapy with children. These children and young people will often have *Specific Difficulties* such as attachment issues, trauma, abuse, ADHD (often known as hyperactivity), autistic spectrum difficulties and selective mutism. This section seeks to fill the gap in understanding and working with children with these kinds of issue.

Some counsellors new to working with children and young people may feel overwhelmed and inadequate for the task. The important thing is for them to ensure that they are adequately supported by their supervisor. Hopefully they will also seek specific training if their growing practice has a large number of, for instance, young clients on the autistic spectrum.

It is OK for the counsellor to say to the child or young person and the parent/carer that they are new to a particular issue and that they will seek clarification and advice through supervision before starting and during the process of therapy. Far better that than launch in with inadequate and possibly unhelpful therapy.

As long as the counsellor is at least one step ahead of the client in terms of understanding the issue, that seems a useful point for starting therapy.

There are likely to be other issues not mentioned here. One of the best ways to learn about how to handle specific difficulties of any sort is to ask – the child or young person and the parent/carer or both. That way therapists show themselves as humble enough to want to learn.

a. Attachment issues

Introduction

A therapist working with children may well come across children and teenagers who have *Attachment Issues.* They may struggle with closeness and feel abandoned. Some will have been fostered or adopted. Others may have had a chaotic upbringing. Still others may have been affected by witnessing domestic violence.

When working with such major issues it is important to consider extra supervision and the counsellor's own personal therapy to deal with internal issues that arise as a result of working with such children and young people.

To understand why people have attachment issues we will look briefly at one method of understanding child development. There are many other models that could be used and each one would probably show something similar.

The theory here is based on Pam Levin-Landheer (1982). She believed there were seven stages:

Being (0 to 6 months) – the child wants to be physically close and develop a loving, sensual and intensely emotional bond with another person. This is the stage when the child is still at one with the mother, then throughout their childhood gradually moves away to independence. If there is no initial bonding or attachment because of abandonment, real or caused by poor parenting, then the child is going to have abandonment issues and may be diagnosed with attachment disorder.

Doing (6 to 18 months) – the period of exploring the world around.

Thinking (18 months to 3 years) – learning independence.

Identity (3 to 6 years) – social relationships, separating fantasy from reality.

Being skilful (6 to 12 years) – exploring tools, skills and values.

Regeneration (13 to 18 years) – discovering sexuality, a personal view on life, a place in the grown-up world.

Recycling (19 years plus) – developing and maintaining relationships, going back and unsticking areas that have been stuck in the person's life.

Much of therapy in general concentrates on the Doing, Thinking, Identity and Being Skilful areas. The focus in this section is on the *Being* stage, which is so often missing for a child or adolescent with attachment or abandonment issues. This is often, though not always, because of poor or missing bonding in the early weeks of life with the primary carer (usually the mother). It can also the result of difficult circumstances that lead up, for instance, to children being fostered or adopted.

A lot has been written and said about the negative effects of attachment issues. These problems include touching inappropriately or not wanting physical contact, control issues, destructiveness and cruelty, problems over food, poor relationships and lack of trust and unhealthy interest in blood, death, fire and sometimes water. What we want to do in this section is to give counsellors working with children and teenagers some tools to help in repairing the damage caused by attachment difficulties and abandonment issues.

The exercise below is designed to help counsellors to understand what it is like to experience being abandoned. This is not only important for counsellors and therapists, it can be helpful for teachers and parents. It is vital that children and young people with attachment and abandonment issues are able to become aware of what it is like. This helps them to contact their real feelings of sadness, anger and even scare.

We strongly recommend that all counsellors wanting to work with children and young people take part themselves in this group activity. This can be done with peers or in group supervision as well as in a training setting. By understanding this vital area and what it feels like, counsellors will be better equipped to help their young clients.

Rescue operation

This attachment/abandonment activity involving a group of people is called *Rescue Operation.* It needs two small mats of equal size. Divide the group into two teams engaged in a Rescue Operation. Each team stands on its own raft (mat). One person from each team is in the imaginary water, acts helpless and seems to be drowning while the team on that side have to decide how to rescue the drowning person safely. The drowning person needs to be far enough away so that the tallest person on that team can't reach them. It is also important to use the *whole* team in the rescue. After all, one person would have to lean out too far and might fall into the water.

It is a good idea to encourage everyone in each team to have a turn at being the drowning person. When the activity is finished the therapist initiates discussion about what it felt like, both as the drowning person and as one of the people on the raft.

When we did this with looked-after children who had both attachment and abandonment issues, they took turns drowning and needing rescuing. Afterwards, these children talked about the familiar feeling of being abandoned and alone while waiting for help.

Therapeutic purpose: Exploring possible attachment and/or abandonment issues in young clients, teamwork, self-awareness.

b. Trauma

Introduction

The theme for this section is *trauma.* Whatever the age of the person, trauma affects every human being deeply. Five months after the Great Fire of London in 1666 the famous diarist Samuel Pepys wrote in his diary: 'It is strange to think how to this very day I cannot sleep a-night without great terrors of the fire; and this very night I could not sleep until two in the morning through thoughts of fire.'

Trauma usually results in sleep difficulties, daydreaming and replaying over and over in the mind what happened. Adults often experience depression, fear and anxiety as a result. When the symptoms last for more than a month, the person is said to have post-traumatic stress disorder (PTSD).

When a child or teenager has been traumatised they will show a range of symptoms. These could include: Anger, panic, sleeplessness, tantrums, agoraphobia, difficult or awkward behaviour, claustrophobia and regression.

Ways to help

Adults tend to want to talk through the traumatic issues they are dealing with. One way of helping adults and some adolescents with PTSD is to get the client to imagine themselves in the event and record what they say in the first person (I, me etc). Then the client plays back the hour-long recording four times a week, imagining the scene, until the client starts to become bored. At that stage they are starting to work through the PTSD. This technique is known as *Imaginal Exposure.*

Children and many young people, on the other hand, have much more natural ways of working through trauma. Playing out the trauma, usually without words and sometimes with plenty of anger, can help them process the event in therapy. They like repetition and this can be used in therapy to help them in repeated creative ways to work through the trauma. Here are some ways that children and young people can use creatively to work through trauma in the counselling room:

- *Drawing.*
- *Clay.*
- *Painting.*
- *Sandtray.*
- *Movement.*
- *Dance.*
- *Anger expression.*

Although aimed mainly at parents, here is a useful website with ideas for helping children who have been traumatised: https://www.helpguide.org/articles/ptsd-trauma/helping-children-cope-with-traumatic-stress.htm

Therapeutic purpose: Activities for children or young people with trauma may need to be repeated many times until the stress subsides. Work with such young clients is often long term but usually very rewarding.

Effects on the therapist

It is important to have extra supervision and personal therapy if necessary when working with children and teenagers who have been traumatised. The reason is that trauma affects the therapist as well as the client.

Judith Herman writes: 'Trauma is contagious. In the role of witness to disaster or atrocity, the therapist is at times emotionally overwhelmed. She experiences, to a lesser degree, the same terror, rage and despair as the patient . . . Hearing the patient's trauma story is bound to revive any personal traumatic experiences that the therapist may have suffered in the past' (Herman, 1992/2015, page 140). Herman also says that this is known as 'traumatic countertransference' or 'vicarious traumatisation'.

Referring to therapists working with children and young people, Clifton Supple writes that the therapist working with a child having symptoms of PTSD may find 'archaic memories revitalised, and the intrusion of the client's trauma into their own waking and sleeping thought processes. The nightmare is shared and both may become incapacitated' (Supple, 2004, page 98).

Important need

While trauma in young clients can be difficult for the therapist, it *can* be dealt with in counselling through care, persistence and attention to any personal issues that come up for the counsellor. The counsellor recognises the difficulties, yet helps the young client in any way possible.

For the child or adolescent client the worst nightmare they have faced can have a happy, positive ending.

c. Abuse

Introduction

This next section is about working with *Abuse.* It's really important that everyone exploring this section or engaged in the activities takes care of themselves. It is probably the most difficult section of all to learn about.

One in five women and one in 20 men are said to have been abused at some time in their childhood. Our belief, based on years of working with abused clients, is that this is likely to be doubled – maybe one in three women and one in ten men. In that case there are likely to be at least three or four students in every school classroom who may have been abused or potentially will be abused in some way!

People who have been abused are usually referred to as *survivors* rather than victims. It is important in counselling to support the child's or young person's abilities to survive rather than see them in a negative way because of what someone has done to them.

Most of the children and young people a counsellor will see who have experienced abuse will have already been referred to social services or been referred to the organisation's safeguarding officer. So in this section we will be exploring ways to help them *creatively.*

Occasionally a counsellor will be the very first person the client under the age of 16 tells about the abuse that is happening or has happened to them. So for a short time we will look at this. It is important to follow most of the guidelines set out by the Crown Prosecution Service for children who may be required to give evidence at some time in the future (see page 182-183).

Below are two examples from private practice to help with this. In both cases the therapist made mistakes and learned from them. We have put questions throughout both examples for the counsellor to consider and perhaps discuss with a supervisor or more experienced counsellor working with children and young people.

Be aware that there are often no cut-and-dried answers. Exploring these kinds of issues before encountering a situation of possible abuse will hopefully equip therapists to give a considered response rather than take a highly emotive, instant reaction that it is not necessarily in the best interest of the child or young person concerned.

Case study one

The therapist was working in a public school when a boy of about 13 started making drawings of stick people with a line between the legs of each person which he said was a penis. At first the counsellor thought that, for a boy in his early teens, there was nothing unusual about the drawings or anything to be concerned about. Then the boy started putting smaller figures beside them, the hands of some of the larger figures touching the penis of the smaller figures.

Questions: Was this abuse? What would you do?

In the next session the boy started talking about the upper house boarders sneaking over at night to do things sexually with the boys in the lower house.

Question: What would you do now?

As a beginning the counsellor spoke to the school's headmaster about their concerns for the boy. The therapist quickly realised this was a big mistake.

Question: What are the potential difficulties of going to the head of a school to talk about possible abuse that was happening within the school?

It was only then that the counsellor took the matter to supervision. The supervisor, who wasn't very experienced in these matters, suggested the therapist speak anonymously to social services and the police to see what they would do. This is the course of action the counsellor took.

Question: What might have been a more useful way of responding to the suggestion of a very inexperienced supervisor?

The counsellor ended up with threats from social services, police, the headmaster and the parent. When the therapist eventually told social services the name of the school, everything had probably been swept under the carpet, the boy had probably been left confused and the young children continued unprotected.

If the counsellor is working with an organisation, including a school, it is very likely that the organisation will have a safeguarding (child protection) liaison officer. In such cases the strong advice is to discuss the matter with the officer concerned at the earliest possible stage. If appropriate the counsellor can make it clear to the officer that they wish to continue working with the client under the guidelines of the Crown Prosecution Service (see pages 182-183).

For therapists who work independently, in addition to supervision it is useful to get advice from an independent specialist agency in matters concerning child protection. CCPAS is a Christian-based organisation staffed by social workers and counsellors. It offers specialist advice on safeguarding issues and confirms the telephone conversation with written recommendations that can be used if the issue were ever to come to court. Their telephone number is 0303 003 1111.

If an independent counsellor decides to contact a local Child Services team direct, it can be extremely helpful to do it on a professional-to-professional basis where the therapist makes clear their continued role rather than hand the matter over to social workers who are unlikely to have the experience of a therapist in working with children. Many Child Services teams have a special application form for a professional to make a referral. In the form the counsellor makes clear their intention to continue therapy with the child or adolescent *within the guidelines of the Crown Prosecution Service* while the investigation is going on.

Case study two
The counsellor was working as part of an organisation with a man. The client said that while he was travelling on the tube train in London, another man had 'accidentally' bumped into him and then touched him sexually.

Question: What would you as the therapist do about that?

The man persuaded the counsellor's client to go home with him and they engaged in sexual acts together on a number of occasions. Often during these sexual acts the other man would show the client photos of choir boys, talking about the sexual activity he had done with them. The boys were from a nationally famous choir.

Question: What would you do now?

The therapist spoke to the organisation's therapeutic supervisor about this. The therapist was told in no uncertain terms that the organisation's policy was not to follow up third-party safeguarding disclosures. Further, he was not to report the matter to social services.

Question: How would you respond, knowing what the therapist knew?

This was not acceptable to the therapist, who took it to specialist children's supervision outside of the organisation. As a result of the advice received the therapist talked with the client and empowered him rather than the therapist to report the matter to police and/or social services. This complied with the organisation's policy and also satisfied the counsellor's conscience.

A year or so later the therapist heard that a paedophile ring involved with that particular choir had been broken up. Perhaps it was partly as a result of the client talking to the authorities.

Our advice in cases such as this is for the counsellor to take their time unless a child is in immediate danger or risk. It is important to seek extra supervision from someone who understands these issues, even if it is only a one-off session, then contact an organisation such as CCPAS (telephone 0303 003 1111) and finally take it forward to police and/or social services, the therapist keeping themselves as the professional who is supporting the child/young person.

Protective shields

Child and teenage survivors who come for therapy may feel helpless, scared, angry, useless or ashamed. Survivors are often more likely to be bullied at school or vulnerable to further abuse. Such clients don't have to accept the negative and usually untrue things people might say about them or the things they might do to them. This is a vital part of the therapy with such children and young people.

In this activity clients are encouraged to produce *Protective Shields* that help them defend against hurtful things. The therapist provides blank pieces of card or paper in the shape of a shield (and other materials in case the client wants to make a shield using a different shape) and encourages clients to use the available art materials to create their own shield.

When the shield is finished, the counsellor initiates discussion about the shield that has been created and how it might be used. For instance, a young client might decide to keep it beside their bed as a form of protection against any bad dreams they might have. They might look at the shield or even hold it up to protect against bad thoughts and feelings about themselves for allowing the abuse to take place. There are many other possible uses of the shield created. It is often useful to explore with children and young people how they see ways the shield can protect them.

This is a useful exercise for children of any age, young people and even for adults.

Therapeutic purpose: Internal protection, helping to develop resilience in survivors.

Power balance

The biggest single issue in abuse of any kind involves the *Power Balance* between abuser and abused (see page 178).

The child sees themselves as the Victim, with the abuser as the Persecutor. The Victim is looking for a Rescuer but is often stopped from seeking help because of threats, shaming and being forced to keep secrets. The object in therapy with children and young people is to restore the power balance, reversing the triangle, with the Survivor on top. Instead of a Rescuer, there is a Helper. In place of a Persecutor there is a Challenger.

Dream house

Young clients who have been abused need help to find a safe place even if their own world (sometimes literally their own house) isn't safe. *Dream House* is an exercise to help child and adolescent clients to understand the significance and importance of finding a house of their imagination. This and similar drawing exercises can be used effectively to help children and young people discover their internal resources in coping with the after-effects of abuse.

The counsellor invites the young client to take a piece of paper and quickly draw their dream house. They are encouraged to set their imagination free and see what results.

It's often useful for the client to draw their dream house with their nondominant hand (left hand if they are right-handed, right hand if they are left-handed). In this way they are using the intuitive side of their brain. Research has shown that this can help to awaken their creative imagination and begin to achieve internally what they have drawn externally.

The counsellor then encourages the client to talk about their dream house if they want to.

Therapeutic purpose: Exploring internal safety, developing resilience and courage, building self-esteem, finding new confidence.

Squeeze and stretch

Children and young people who have been abused, particularly sexually, frequently lose some of the awareness of their body. For them this was originally a way of protecting themselves from what was happening to their bodies. There are lots of physical activities that can help an abused child or teenager start to become aware of their own body again without feeling threatened.

This exercise is called *Squeeze and Stretch.* Before starting, the therapist will need to assure the young client that they can stop the activity at any time they want if they feel uncomfortable. This acts as a counter to the original abuse which was almost always without the child's permission.

This activity can help the client learn the difference between tension and relaxation. First, the child or young person sits on a chair – or, even better, lies on the floor – and relaxes all their muscles, letting their whole body go floppy. If the client has difficulty doing this, the counsellor can break it down into parts of the body. 'Relax your head and neck. [PAUSE] Now relax your chest and tummy. [PAUSE] Let your legs and feet go floppy.'

The power balance in abuse

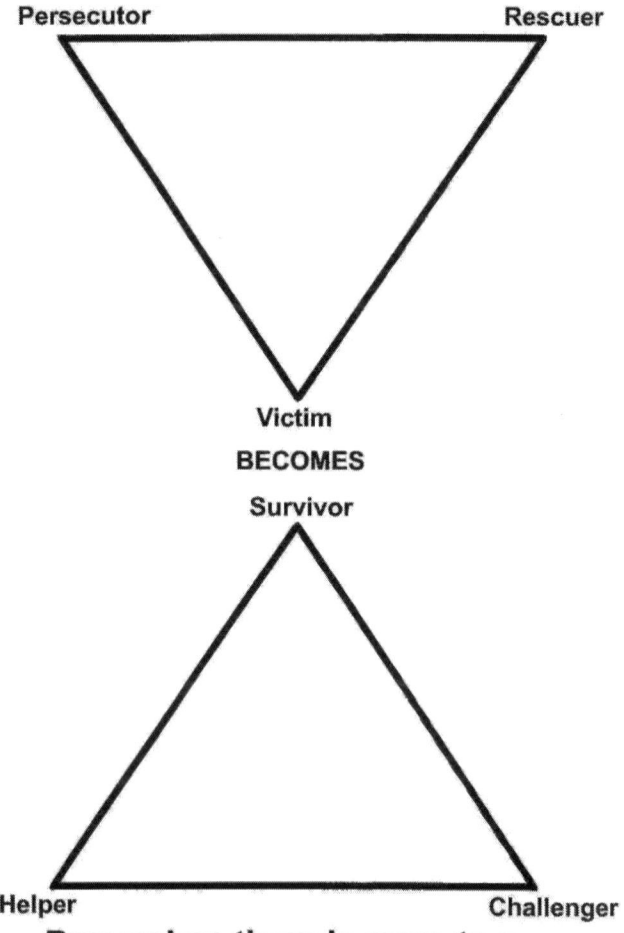

Persecutor · Rescuer

Victim

BECOMES

Survivor

Helper · Challenger

Remember, there is more to a client than just being a survivor

adapted from Don Morris, ITA Conference papers 9/4/1999

The therapist waits a few seconds and then invites the child or young person to squeeze tightly, arms around their knees and backs arched. They hold this position for several seconds and can be encouraged to squeeze even tighter until their muscles start to shake. Then they relax and stretch out their whole body, relaxing all their muscles, releasing the tension in their joints.

This can be done several times until it seems appropriate to stop.

While it would be interesting to discuss how the child or young person felt doing that exercise, it is probably better to move on to something else without discussion. This will no doubt seem safer to the child or teenage client who has been abused at the hands of an adult or older child.

Therapeutic purpose: Stress relief, understanding the body and bodily control, relaxation in a safe environment.

Marbles and me

Marbles and Me is an activity for a client that the counsellor knows or believes has been abused. Remember, a counsellor can work with clients under the age of 16 who have been abused and who are due to give evidence in court as long as neither the therapist nor the client talks directly about the abuse.

In this activity the counsellor and client work together. The client is invited to take a handful of marbles, though any similar objects can be used. They place the marbles in front of them to show their life – the good things and the bad things. Once they have done this, with the encouragement of the counsellor, they remove the good things one by one, saying what they are.

Now they have only the bad things of their childhood so far. The client does not have to say what these bad things are. The counsellor invites the client to have a look at the marbles representing the bad things, then says things to the client such as:

Most people would never have wanted you to go through those horrible things. They would have wanted you to have a happy, carefree life. Yet even the bad things that have happened have helped you be the kind of person you are today. You wouldn't have the strengths and abilities to cope if you hadn't suffered. Your tears and pain have made you the [lovely, likeable, friendly, caring] person you are now.

Finally, the counsellor suggests that the client look at the good things and the bad things together. They make up who they are today. This is their life so far.

After the activity the counsellor and client can talk together about what it was like for the client to play the *Marbles and Me* game.

Therapeutic purpose: Exploring the positives in life to counteract the negatives as a result of real or possible abuse in the past.

Working with abusers

Before finishing this section on abuse, we want to consider family work with abuse. A common belief is that people who have been abused are more vulnerable to becoming abusers, though research shows this is unlikely. With that thought in mind, is it possible also to work with people who hurt children physically, sexually or emotionally? We realise this is a very sensitive and controversial subject – and it is definitely not for every therapist.

First, there are different categories of abusers. There are, for instance, *children who abuse younger children,* usually in a sexual way. Toni Johnson (1999) points out that 40 to 85 per cent of all children engage in some sort of sexual behaviour before the age of 13. Most of this activity can be considered normal and healthy sexual exploration. When it becomes abusive, there are usually reasons such as being home alone for long periods, surfing the internet without supervision, or over-exposure to sexuality in the home. Such children and young people respond well to therapy from a therapist who is caring yet also has clear boundaries.

Abuse within the family, provided it has stopped and any necessary legal steps taken, can also be dealt with in therapy. Rita & Blair Justice (1975) suggest working with couples where one partner was a former abuser. They take the view that child abuse within a family is the result of unhealthy symbiosis. The non-abusing partner often stands by passively, even though she instinctively knows what is happening.

Children and the court system

Occasionally a counsellor might work with a client who may be asked to give evidence in court, usually about abuse. Here is a brief summary of the Crown Prosecution Service (CPS) guidelines on such therapy:

■ *Make the police and CPS aware that therapy is taking place.*

■ *Therapy must be individual rather than group because of possible influence by other group members.*

■ *Avoid leading questions and discussing details of the allegations. Steer clear of language that could be considered as instructing the witness.*

■ *Keep careful notes of each session, with date, time and who was present. Transcriptions of all that is said aren't needed.*

■ *Offer limited confidentiality. What happens in the sessions doesn't need sharing unless it is directly relevant to criminal proceedings.*

■ *If the child talks about their experiences the counsellor can offer general assurance and support but should not encourage the client to talk more about what happened.*

■ *Should any new investigations be needed, the therapy can continue without disruption. Such decisions, however, may be made at a multi-disciplinary meeting that includes the therapist.*

■ *A prosecutor may advise that therapy could prejudice the criminal case. Therapy may still be in the best interests of the child. The therapist then assures the prosecutor that in the sessions the child didn't say anything inconsistent with their original statement to the police.*

These guidelines apply to England and Wales. Other countries may have a similar policy. For full information about these guidelines see: https://www.cps.gov.uk/legal-guidance/therapy-provision-therapy-child-witnesses-prior-criminal-trial

d. ADHD

Introduction

This section explores working with children and teenagers who have been diagnosed or labelled with *ADHD – Attention-Deficit/Hyperactivity Disorder.*

This is a controversial label mainly, it would seem, because some children who have no proper boundaries at home get an ADHD diagnosis. Others may be attention-seeking because of environmental issues such as the breakdown of the family.

Symptoms of true ADHD according to the psychiatric manual DSM-V (American Psychiatric Association, 2013) include inattention, hyperactivity and impulsivity.

Inattention could include: inability to concentrate, doesn't seem to listen, fails to finish schoolwork, difficulty organising tasks, easily distracted, forgets everyday activities.

Hyperactivity and impulsivity could include: fidgeting, can't sit still, runs about or climbs excessively, can't play quietly, on the go as if driven by a motor, blurts out answers before questions have been finished, difficulty waiting their turn, often interrupts or intrudes on others' conversations.

The child or young person with true ADHD is often treated by a psychiatrist with a brain stimulating drug such as methylphenidate (Ritalin) or, less popular in the UK, dextroamphetamine, which was once known as the street drug Purple Hearts. The idea is that stimulating the brain can help the child or young person control their impulsive and hyperactive behaviour. The drugs certainly help, though they aren't the complete answer and they can sometimes have unwanted side effects.

Therapists working with children and young people who have ADHD need to check regularly and carefully what the client is eating and drinking – especially if symptoms suddenly get worse. Many foods and drinks have chemicals, preservatives, caffeine and excess sugar that could make the behaviour worse.

Counselling can work well with children and adolescents who have ADHD, though the counsellor will need to be ready to adapt when things seem to get out of hand.

The counsellor was running their first therapy group. It included a boy who had been diagnosed with ADHD and another who was on the autistic spectrum with what was known at the time as Asperger's.

One of the activities for the group's first session was creating shapes on the table using dried beans. All was going well until the boy with ADHD suddenly decided to start throwing his beans around. Before the therapist could do anything about it, the whole group started throwing beans around the room.

The activity had been ruined because of hyperactivity. On reflection the therapist could have used the bean-throwing as an activity in its own right, encouraging all the children to find their freedom in expression. At the time, though, the therapist merely wanted to give up being a counsellor!

The positive note in this initial group session was that the boy with autistic tendencies volunteered to vacuum up the beans at the end of the session. Using his focus on detail he made sure every single bean was cleared up.

The therapist learned that it was possible to harness for good what many people considered the negative aspects in children with hyperactivity and those children on the autistic spectrum. It was a valuable lesson to learn for future therapeutic work with children.

When working with children and young people who have ADHD it is important to realise that they have difficulty with changing their inappropriate behaviour without external intervention. They also struggle with giving themselves self-praise for good, appropriate behaviour. So it is useful to combine fun activities in which they learn self-control with praise for success.

Norma Leben in *Directive Group Play Therapy* (Leben, 2000) stresses the importance of giving young children with

ADHD external reinforcers – stickers, tokens, praise for attempts and success. She writes: 'In the end, the child hopefully will have positive behaviours and the ability to learn and maintain these behaviours through self-praise/self-evaluation.'

Floating in space

Floating in Space is one activity that can help a child of any age to gain control and have fun. It is important to remember to include plenty of praise and encouragement for trying – and of course for success.

The children or young people are invited to imagine themselves as astronauts about to go on a zero gravity walk outside the spaceship. The clients could begin by lying on the floor and then, when the music starts, move to standing up. If the therapist is working with a group, one particular rule is useful, especially if they all have ADHD tendencies: They are to make sure they don't bang into each other, *accidentally or on purpose.*

When the music starts they start their space walk in time to the music, the therapist taking part as well if at all possible.

As they float in space, moving in time to the music, the children or young people can be invited to look round and say something positive about the movements of someone near to them. If it is just the counsellor and the young client, the counsellor initiates saying something positive to the client and invites a similar positive comment from the client.

When the music finishes, the child/children could lie on the floor, eyes closed, and just relax. The music we recommend for this activity is by Kitaro and is called *Space II.* Counsellors could of course use any kind of music that suits their practice and clients.

Therapeutic purpose: Helping children and young people to understand themselves and their bodies, learning control and having plenty of fun doing it.

Grounding

A useful way to help children and teenagers with ADHD is to enable them to find fun ways for *Grounding* themselves. Far from being a parental punishment, grounding in a therapeutic context is a positive way to calm down and reduce any anxiety they feel. In that sense it can be useful for most young clients, not just those with issues around hyperactivity.

The child or young person will probably find sitting or lying down more helpful than standing up. Many children will naturally want to close their eyes for elements of this activity, though we recommend this as optional. Here are a few phrases for positive grounding that the therapist can offer to young clients:

■ *Imagine a favourite place where you've been on holiday or where you could imagine you have been.*
■ *Give yourself a hug, squeezing tightly until you feel calmer.*
■ *Breathe as deeply as you can.* [To assist in this the therapist could produce bubble pots and suggest they use their breath to blow bubbles, or they could be offered coloured feathers to blow along a set course.]
■ *Tense up your muscles as much as you can, hold for the count of five, then relax them again.*

Children/young people could be invited to suggest other ways to help themselves calm down when they are at home. The counsellor may want to write down the best of these and then ask the child's permission to use their ideas with other children or young people who struggle to relax.

Therapeutic purpose: Reduction of anxiety, managing stress, developing self-control, combating anxiety.

I am a tree

The exercise *I Am a Tree* is one often used on drama courses. It is also useful in therapy, especially to help children and teenagers with ADHD to learn control and the slowing down of their bodies.

Young clients start by crouching as low as they can, curling up on the floor to imagine they are acorns. It is useful to have gentle music playing in the background. We have used tracks from Dan Gibson's album *English Country Garden,* though any gentle music is helpful.

As the music starts to build, the therapist invites children or young people to start growing from the acorn, very slowly. Perhaps one hand goes up slowly, moving back and forth as it grows through the soil, followed by the other hand. Then the head raises followed slowly by the body.

Eventually the young client is standing up, 'branches' (arms) fully outstretched and 'leaves' (fingers) waving in the breeze.

At each stage the therapist encourages slow 'growth' in the same way that the oak is a slow-growing tree.

At the end of the activity it is often useful to discuss with the child or young person what it was like being the acorn growing into the oak tree.

Therapeutic purpose: Confidence and self-awareness, understanding one's own capabilities, learning to slow down with control.

e. Autistic spectrum difficulties

Introduction

Increasingly, child and teenage clients present for therapy showing symptoms of mild autism. Some of them will almost certainly have what used to be called Asperger's. The phrase usually used for these conditions is Autistic Spectrum Difficulties or ASD. ASD covers everything from the boy totally engrossed ('lost') in his computer game, to the highly intelligent child with 'Asperger's', to the child with severe learning difficulties who lives in a world of his own with no eye contact at all. Most but not all children with ASD are boys. Interestingly, at least in our view, most men and boys sometimes show some mild tendencies towards ASD.

Children of any age with ASD usually have three things:

■ *Difficulty in social interaction – they struggle to make and keep friends and they find it difficult to maintain eye contact.*
■ *Difficulty in social communication – they often can't understand other people's gestures, facial expressions and tone of voice.*
■ *Difficulty in using their imagination.*

They also often have repetitive patterns of behaviour and resistance to change.

When working with children and young people showing symptoms of ASD it is important to ensure that the activities are *structured.* One way of doing this is through creating pathways of communication – activities that lead naturally from one to the other. This is especially useful for young clients on the autistic spectrum. These pathways of communication are important for children and young people who have more significant forms of ASD. Rather than invite them to do something completely different, the therapist observes what they are already doing and seeks to develop it from there (see pages 191-192).

Children on the autistic scale may tend to drift into their own world. There is usually nothing to worry about when this happens. Maybe the child or young person needs some time simply to be themselves.

The client was in his first year of secondary school and wasn't coping very well with the transition from a smaller school where teachers had understood him. He resented the recent diagnosis by a clinical psychiatrist that he was on the autistic spectrum. The word 'Asperger's' had been used, and he hated the label. 'Why can't I be ordinary?' he pleaded with the counsellor.

The therapy was to help him deal with his new condition and to find coping strategies.

During the sessions the client started enjoying seeing his 'problem' as merely a different way of thinking from everyone else. The counsellor had suggested that his way of thinking was the right way up and the thinking of most other people was upside down. The young client was delighted with the idea, and this became his theme at home, at school and in the sessions.

He couldn't manage to come to any of the sessions without a member of his family with him, usually his mother or grandmother. However, his socialising skills had increased dramatically. Therapy had enabled him at least partly to accept his ASD diagnosis.

Sticker for eye contact

Clients with autistic spectrum difficulties and others with anxiety such as those with selective mutism often have difficulty making eye contact. Most other people don't identify lack of eye contact but just think there is something strange about the person without knowing what it really is.

One of the first steps for the therapist working with such young child clients is to help them imitate eye contact so they are seen as socially accepted. Adults and teenagers may be able to imagine looking at the triangle shape at the top of the nose.

For young children on the autistic spectrum, *a Sticker for Eye Contact* is a useful way to help them learn the skill. A small sticker is placed at the top of the nose of both client and therapist. The child is encouraged to look at that sticker rather than into the eyes. The therapist can do the same, assuring the client that they are not staring into the client's eyes. With practice, the sticker can be left out and the client can learn to do this on a regular basis with friends at school and even strangers.

Staring at people is also not acceptable socially. Normally a person looks away every 20 seconds or so. This needs explaining as well, with opportunity to practice. The idea is to look at the sticker again, look away every 20 seconds or so and then look straight back.

Remember, though, a child or teenager with ASD may interpret this literally and look away precisely every 20 seconds! If so, a bit more work together may be needed.

Therapeutic purpose: Enabling a young client on the autistic spectrum to cope in what they perceive as an upside-down world, a fun and relatively safe activity.

Play strategies

In therapy with all young clients it is important to emphasise the vital importance of child-initiated play. This is even more important when the counsellor is working with children and young people who have communication difficulties, such as those with ASD.

Dr Shoshana Levin Fox, a psychologist and play therapist who is based in Jerusalem, Israel, believes that it is important for the young child to take the initiative, and not try to steer the child into what the adult wants. In a workshop presentation (Levin Fox, 2005) she proposed three strategies:

■ *Use toys with appeal and novelty.*
■ *Follow the child's lead and join their play to create circles of communication. Wait until the child gives an indication they want more, for example the boy with ASD standing on a low bench bends his knees and only then does the therapist hold out their hands to catch him.*
■ *Emphasise play that involves shared fun (such as chasing, hide-and-seek with objects or the actual person).*

Although children and young people with ASD and those with selective mutism tend to isolate themselves, it is important to enter their world, even when they don't appear interested. 'The chromosome does not have the last word,' Levin Fox says. Her key tips are:

■ *Talk a lot to the child during play.*
■ *Encourage ideas for pretend play.*
■ *Use the child's obsessions to help break into their world in order to help them.*
■ *Add characters and create problems in the play.*

Levin Fox has had remarkable success with her work, including helping children with autistic tendencies as young as 18 months or two years old. While playing with a young child with communication difficulties she has the following suggestions for the therapist:

■ **Think developmentally** – *maybe even going back over the stages.*
■ **Think senses** – *needing more or less sensory stimulation.*
■ **Think active** – *remember, lively activities are best.*
■ **Think baby play time** – *often children need earlier stages.*
■ **Think challenge** – *needing activities that are not easy.*
■ **Think meaning** – *why they behave in the way they do.*
■ **Think 'don't give up'** – *keep inputting even when it seems hopeless.*
■ **Think someone's home** – *they are seen as a problem in their family.*
■ **Think symbolic** – *how does their behaviour symbolise underlying issues?*
■ **Think eclectic** – *use every possible strategy to break through barriers.*

It is important to remember that children on the autistic spectrum find it difficult to use imagination and metaphor so stick whenever possible with 'concrete' vocabulary (words that are direct, clear and free of metaphor).

Focusing using chopsticks

It is clear that communication is not just about speaking. It is about watching, listening, and using empathy and intuition. All these can help to meet the needs of the young client with ASD tendencies.

Focusing on Chopsticks is a nonintrusive, safe and fun exercise in focusing that can assist in communication between therapist and client, including working with children's therapy groups. If the therapist is working with an individual, they each take a chopstick. Then they use a finger each to hold the chopstick between them. Once one chopstick is in place, they use a finger each to hold the other chopstick.

Together they try some movements up and down and in circles. The focus is on keeping the chopsticks from falling down rather than looking at each other. Children and young people with ASD tend to love this exercise because of the attention to detail and the skill involved in succeeding.

Similar activities using chopsticks can be done in a therapy group. Each person has one chopstick and joins with the person beside them. Eventually the whole group is joined in a circle of chopsticks. Moving the chopsticks together without dropping them can be an even bigger challenge.

Therapeutic purpose: Focusing on an activity such as this is helpful for young clients on the autistic spectrum who are often bombarded by too much information. A fun activity that can be done again and again.

Further ideas

One thing counsellors can do with children and young people who have ASD and struggle with understanding emotions is to collect pictures of faces from magazines and help the child relate the shape of the mouth and eyes to the emotion being expressed.

Other ideas relate to sensory awareness. Certain kinds of wrapping paper are reflective and see-through and can provide pleasure for a child or young person on the autistic spectrum. The same applies to a flashing ball that can help with sensory stimulation.

f. Selective mutism

Introduction

Young children who struggle to speak at home or at school are said to have **selective mutism.** Selective mutism according to DSM-V is 'consistent failure to speak in specific social situations in which there is an expectation for speaking (eg at school) despite speaking in other situations' (American Psychiatric Association, 2013). Children with it often use gestures or noises with their mouth. It is believed to be caused by severe anxiety resulting in an over-reaction in the amygdala of the brain. The reaction has been compared to the involuntary reaction a baby makes in a fearful situation, but in selective mutism the brain responds even when the child is not in danger.

Children with the condition often have raised sensory awareness, separation anxiety and introspection. They might wet the bed even when everything seems fine. On the positive side they are often highly creative and work well in therapy. The goal of therapy is to lower their anxiety through raising their self-esteem and their confidence in social settings.

The 10-year-old client, who had numerous anxieties, didn't speak at home or at school. The therapist had never before worked with a child having selective mutism but quickly learned to understand the client's gestures and made-up sign language. It was obvious to the therapist that the client knew what he needed to do in therapy, so it was a case of following the client's lead.

There was a large cardboard box in the therapy room and client pointed to it, gesturing that he wanted to get into it. The therapist helped him do so. Then the client showed through signs that he wanted the box closed with the therapist holding the lid down.

A few seconds later the client suddenly pushed up the flaps and burst out of the box in a dramatic gesture. He was smiling and obviously happy, with the occasional quiet squeak of delight rather than the expected laughter.

A couple of sessions later the therapist found out from the parent that the young client had had a long-term fear of closed and tight spaces. It was clear that bursting out the cardboard box was the client's way of helping himself to resolve this issue.

Communication game

Part of the skill of understanding a child with selective mutism is learning to communicate without words. *Communication Game* is an exercise in nonverbal communication skills. One person tries to communicate with their partner what they had to eat last night, but can't speak. The person listening doesn't try to help.

Then they swap around and the other person again tries to communicate with their partner.

Now the first person communicates again about what they ate last night, this time their partner listening and watching carefully, looking for clues and helping as much as they can. The second person looks for gestures, noises, arm movements and facial expressions.

How did the person who couldn't speak feel? The pair/s discuss this and other elements of this exercise.

Therapeutic purpose: This is an activity for trainees to learn how to work with young children who have selective mutism.

19
Health and safety

Counsellors working with children and young people in private practice or setting up their own organisation will be expected to have a Health & Safety Policy in place. We have included in Appendix C a sample of the policy we used in our practice. Counsellors are free to use this as a template for their therapy practice or their organisation.

If the counsellor is working for another organisation or offering their services to a school, for instance, it is important for the organisation to have your own policies. As someone who is employed or subcontracted to the organisation the counsellor is strongly recommended to read and make a note of the basic principles contain in the policy. If there is no policy in place it seems sensible to offer help to the organisation so that they get one in place as soon as possible.

Even if it seems routine and not necessary, people expect organisations and individuals to have thought through issues around health and safety.

Health

It is vital to ensure the continued good health of young clients while they are in the therapy room.

We recommend at intake that, in addition to contact details, the name and contact details of the client's general practitioner are recorded, in case of a sudden emergency.

It is also very important to ask about the young client's health issues. For instance, without this knowledge a child with asthma may have an asthma attack that could be perceived as something much more serious, resulting in an ambulance being called when an inhaler may be the initial response.

If in exceptional circumstances the counsellor intends to offer any sort of refreshments to young clients, such as in group work, it is vital to check for any allergies to avoid unhelpful or even dangerous food or drink. This check can easily be done at intake.

Another useful question to ask is about any medication that the child or young person takes. Some medicines, such as those prescribed for psychological problems, could have an effect on the therapy. A quick discussion with the specialist supervisor about a medication a new client is taking could help the counsellor new to working with this age group.

Safety

Client safety

The therapy room needs to be safe and reasonably free from hazards. We recommend doing a risk assessment and writing up a short report to keep in the file in case of any questions about safety.

Toys and other objects need looking at carefully to avoid too many objects with sharp edges. When a plastic object breaks it often has very sharp edges and it may then need throwing away. Hopefully such breakages will be minimised by including 'care for property' as part of the initial rules at the beginning of therapy. When working with very young children it is important to avoid tiny items such as marbles that could result in choking if swallowed.

Having said that, there will always be a small element of risk when a therapy room contains a large number of play items. This is an acceptable part of working therapeutically with children and young people. It is important, however, when renewing professional indemnity insurance to tell the insurance company that the therapy room contains play items. Then at least they can keep a note of that fact. If they are reluctant to insure on that basis, there are plenty of other companies that are happy to include in their insurance policy creative items in the therapy room.

When working outdoors there are other safety factors for the counsellor or therapist to consider. Depending on the activities planned, children/young people may trip or graze their knee. It is useful to carry a small first-aid kit when organising therapy outside the therapy room.

Again, it is important to do a risk assessment in advance to minimise the possibility of injury.

Safety of the counsellor

Counsellors working with young clients, especially with teenagers and older children, will need to consider their own safety as well as that of the young clients.

Having a clear initial agreement about 'respect for self and other people' will certainly help. If at some point in a session a client becomes agitated or extremely angry, a quick reminder about that agreement can be useful in helping to diffuse the agitation.

It is also useful to consider external support if things become difficult or unsafe. A good policy is always to ensure that there is someone else in the same building while counselling is happening. Having some sort of panic button is also extremely important. The panic button could be wired into the building or the counsellor could bring in with them a handheld screech alarm in the unlikely event that it is needed.

20
Small world

Introduction

Small world activities can be used in therapy with an individual or a group. Small world objects can be used in all kinds of situations. A small box or bag of objects can go with the counsellor anywhere and they can be used effectively in any situation with children or adults. Using small world objects it is possible to do therapy in the tiniest space.

They don't necessarily have to be toys – whatever the therapist has with them at the time can be used in this kind of special play.

Small world objects are ideal when a child is ill or dying or when the therapist doesn't have enough space, such as going into a sick child's home. They can be used on a small bit of floor space, a tiny part of the bedside table or even a tray on the lap of the child.

For children and young people who are terminally ill or dying, small world objects provide the ideal opportunity to solve whatever problems they need to solve as life reaches its conclusion for them.

Giant diamond

For the activity *Giant Diamond* the counsellor will need a large diamond-shaped crystal. The crystal is passed to the young client with words such as: 'Imagine this crystal is a giant diamond and say what you would do if you had a diamond this size.'

If there is a therapy group they can pass it round and each say what they would do with such a valuable diamond.

Answers usually vary from 'Sell it and make lots of money' to 'Use it to help poor people' and everything in between. Every answer is acceptable.

Once the activity is finished suggest that clients comment on what it was like to hold such a valuable pretend diamond. It might also be useful to ask them to comment on their answer.

Therapeutic purpose: Helping children to explore what they value most; within a group setting understanding other people's perspective.

Creating families in small world

In this exercise young clients will be able to create their own family using small world objects. The idea of *Creating Families in Small World* is that clients can create their family exactly as they would like it to be, using whatever materials they want to use. Once clients have created their family they can be invited to move the family around and put each family member in whatever position they like.

When the child or young person has finished creating their family the counsellor can talk about the family as shown by the objects. It isn't necessary to engage in long conversations about each family member. Instead the therapist observes the positions and type of objects used for each family member.

Therapeutic purpose: *Enabling the client to understand their family and how they (the client) fits into it. Celebrating positive elements of the family. Understanding visually any problems within the family.*

My jewels

What are the things that are precious to a child or teenage client? In this exercise the client take three or four 'jewels' (for instance, glass beads usually used in floral displays) and then tells the therapist what each of the jewels represents.

The object of this activity is to help young clients identify and own the positive things in their lives that will sustain them during difficult times. If a child or young person doesn't think they have any jewels the counsellor and client can explore together how they can identify jewels for themselves.

Therapeutic purpose: *Self-esteem, finding positives in life when things are difficult, exploring resources the client already has.*

My life now

One of the skills needed for someone using therapy with children and young people is imagination. That imagination can be used to help the children they work with. As 70 per cent of children who come for therapy are boys, it is important to be good at working with cars and trucks, which boys often favour. Girls tend to use animals to represent families, themselves and life experiences. While these statements may appear generalising, it is a common experience that boys and girls gravitate in this way at a difficult point in their lives when they come into therapy.

My Life Now is an exercise about using vehicles that girls as well as boys may find helpful. Here is a proposed way of wording it when working with a group:

Think of what your life is like right now. Are you rushing along, or going slow? Are you taking risks? Are you broken down or going steadily along the road? Find a partner and take turns showing without any words what your life is like right now. You can use one or several toy vehicles to show this. The person watching remains silent. At the end of three minutes you can talk together about what you have made. Then swap around and the other person do the same.

If the counsellor is working with an individual, they invite the client to take part in the activity, then talk about it. If appropriate, the counsellor can then do the activity with the young client watching on. It is important for the counsellor to reveal personal information only to the extent that it is therapeutically beneficial to the client.

Therapeutic purpose: *Understanding what stage the client is at, exploring any areas where the client is 'broken down' and needs fixing.*

Magic box

For this activity the therapist will need an empty box, possibly gift-wrapped, known as the *Magic Box.* The client is invited to pretend that it contains things that are very special to them. If working with a group, the box is passed around and each young client imagines that the box contains something they really want to have. Each client tells the rest of the group what it would be.

The box is then again passed to the client or around the group. This time each client imagines the box could contain one person past or present they would really like to meet. Who would it be?

Finally, they hold the box and imagine it contains something that they want to give to a person that they love or like. What would it be? Who would they give it to?

Therapeutic purpose: Imagination, focus on what matters to the young client, a fun activity that moves from self to others as it goes along.

Yarn drawing: Cooperation

In the *Yarn Drawing: Cooperation* exercise a young client uses part of a ball of wool to make a drawing on the floor in front of them. They describe what they have made and then passes the ball back to the counsellor or, in the case of a group, to the next person. As they do this they put a foot on the end of their 'drawing' while the counsellor or the next person has a turn. If the counsellor is working with only one client they can take turns or make a circle of pictures.

Once everyone has had a turn the therapist can invite the group (or the individual child) to look at the whole picture. Together they describe what they see.

The group leader might ask: What letters of the alphabet can you see? What shapes do you see? What numbers do you see? What kind of people do you see and what are they doing?

Therapeutic purpose: *Encouraging cooperation, enhancing creativity, helping with diagnosis and assessment and developing confidence.*

Pipe-cleaner connections

Coloured pipe-cleaners can be used to shape a family member. Then the family members can be joined together in the way that the attachment is seen by the child. The activity *Pipe Cleaner Connections* provides important information on attachments and what is known as appropriate and unhealthy symbiosis. Healthy symbiosis is where, for instance, a child is deeply attached to a parent yet has their own life as well. Unhealthy symbiosis has been defined as 'a relationship in which two or more individuals behave as though between them they form a single person' (Stewart & Joines, 1987, page 334).

Part of therapy with children and young people can be understanding their attachments and breaking any unhealthy and unhelpful symbioses. The client may represent this visually during the course of therapy by gradually attaching the pipe-cleaners together to form the healthy attachments or undoing the pipe-cleaners until they have become autonomous.

Therapeutic purpose: Enabling the child or young person to understand in a visual way family and other connections that may be healthy and helpful and those that at present may be unhelpful. Making changes to the pipe-cleaner figures as the sessions go by may represent actual changes in the child's relationships that are occurring outside of the therapy room.

Toy soldiers: Protection and personal safety

When we have asked children and young people from places such as Serbia and Romania, and even in the UK, what comes to mind when they think about soldiers they often associate them with war, uniforms, guns, battles and active defence of their country. These are all important parts of the soldier's work. In *Toy Soldiers: Protection and Personal Safety,* though, we are looking at soldiers in terms of *protection.*

The counsellor invites the child or adolescent client to think of the elements of internal protection they have. It might be the message in their head to look before they cross the road or to avoid putting their hand into a fire. Younger children may need some prompting to get to the answers.

For each protection that children identify, they put a toy soldier down on the floor around them. The soldier faces outwards, away from them, to protect them from harm or danger.

After a number of soldiers are in place around the client (with prompting from the therapist if needed), the counsellor and client discuss what it feels like to be in the middle of this protection. How safe do they feel? What is it like knowing that they already have some inbuilt protection and can add more when they are ready?

Therapeutic purpose: *Exploring the client's internal protection in a visual and often powerful way, realising the importance of self-protection.*

Bean shapes

In *Bean Shapes* children or young people are passed a jar of dried beans. They take a handful of the beans and make a shape from them. Once they have finished, the therapist looks at what is created, seeks to understand it and validates the creative effort, even if it is difficult to understand. They simply ask for clarification. In this exercise, validation, encouragement and acceptance are very important.

If the counsellor is working with an individual, the client and counsellor could each make a shape and discuss what they have created.

For a therapy group the counsellor could get the participants to make three shapes, going round each time to ask them to make another shape. After each shape is completed get the person (you included) to describe it.

Finally, they can look at the three shapes and see how they might relate together. It is important to remember validation of the clients' efforts.

Therapeutic purpose: *An exercise designed to encourage confidence and build self-esteem through genuine validation and appreciation.*

Roger & Christine Day

21
Client notes

It is important to keep notes or *client summary sheets* on each session with a child, young person or family. But what form is it best to keep these notes?

First, it is vital to recognise that therapy notes on a person under the age of 16 can't necessarily be confidential. A parent or carer could demand to read the notes, and the counsellor will be expected to comply. The courts or the police could also demand to read them.

Client codes

With these factors in mind, it is important to organise client summary sheets so that any legal demands to have access to them won't compromise the ongoing therapy with the child or young person.

Our recommendation is to have a *code name or number* for each client and put this at the top of each page of the client summary sheet. The client's personal information (name, address, date of birth etc) is kept separate, and a third index card then links the client's name with the code used on the client notes.

Computer or handwritten?

It has happened on more than one occasion that a young client has become the subject of a course case and court officials have ceased all computers on the therapist's premises. To avoid clients' notes being treated in such a disrespectful way, we recommend that nothing is kept on a computer. Although this may seem antiquated, it could avoid the negative effect of a possible raid on the counsellor's computer.

We recommend keeping *handwritten notes* where possible. If a computer is used, the notes can be printed off, the history is then wiped off and no file kept. The same would apply to the code name or number and the index card linking the notes to the code name or number. Each of these could be handwritten.

Notes versus personal journal

The contents of the notes also need to be considered carefully. We strongly recommend sticking only to a *brief factual description* of what takes place in the therapy room. Here is a suggested approach:

Client AA1 spent time creating a city in the sandtray. He then moved on to creating music with a tambourine and a small drum. He hit the punchbag several times. Then he talked about a time and place when he felt safe and comfortable. In the future he wants to sleep at night without having nightmares.

Any *personal thoughts and suppositions* on the part of the counsellor are best kept in a personal journal that by its nature can't be used by the courts. It can, however, be taken to supervision and discussed there, though it is best to keep supervision notes brief and factual.

All this might seem extreme. Yet counselling notes can on occasion be required by the authorities. In a 23-year history of counselling and psychotherapy Roger had two occasions when his counselling notes were taken. In one case the adult client had signed permission for them to be made available to police officers. In the other case the courts required the notes, a written report and the presence in court of Roger as an expert witness concerning his child client.

In both cases the notes had been carefully written to keep to facts rather than speculation. And, as a qualified professional, Roger was able to charge a considerable amount for the release of the notes and the subsequent interview he gave to the police and his presence in court as an expert witness.

Summary sheet

A suggested client summary sheet for working with children, young people and families is included in Appendix E. The counsellor is free to use this or to develop their own summary sheet. The important details to include are the age of the children, the types of creative work used (if appropriate) and a signature from their supervisor, who must have training and/or experience in working with children or creativity.

22
Russian dolls in therapy

Introduction

Russian dolls – correctly known as matryoshtas – provide many powerful ways to help clients, old and young, with their emotional difficulties. It is best to have a set of about five dolls. When buying them it is useful to check the smaller ones and choose those that show expressions such as sadness or anger as these are more effective in therapy. Our experience is that secondhand matryoshkas often have better features than the brand new mass-produced ones.

It is important to note that matryoshkas must be kept away from sandtrays. Once sand has got into the connecting collars the dolls are extremely difficult ever to use again.

For more about using matryoshkas with clients see our book *Matryoshkas in Therapy: Creative ways to use Russian dolls with clients* (Day & Day, 2014).

Making changes

Making Changes is one of the simpler activities when working with matryoshkas. The counsellor introduces the matryoshkas to their young client, explaining that the set is composed of smaller dolls who, because of life experiences, have made up the present (largest) doll.

The counsellor invites their client to open up and explore the set of Russian dolls and set them out on a flat surface. The client is told that positive and negative things happen to all of us that mould and shape our characters. Many things may have occurred at different times for these dolls, and together those things make up the person the client is today.

The client is encouraged to talk about some of these things that have happened to the smaller dolls and how they have affected the largest doll. Then the counsellor asks what changes the client would like to make with the largest doll during the therapy. The client is reminded that the past cannot be changed. What *can* be changed is how the doll deals with situations now and in the future.

The counsellor discusses practically how these changes can be made and how they will affect the doll. As with other activities, the counsellor needs to be ready to use this activity over several sessions, even returning to it after a time.

Therapeutic purpose: Using a set of inanimate objects (matryoshkas) to explore a young client's life so far, good and not so good, and enabling them to focus on the here-and-now and moving positively towards the future.

The trainee was a man who was working with what appeared to be a female set of dolls. Despite this, he chose repeatedly to use the words 'he' and 'him' throughout the exercise, so the facilitator followed the trainee's lead.

As each doll was revealed, the facilitator asked: 'What age is he now?' and then: 'How is he feeling and thinking?'

When the trainee reached the second from smallest doll he said the age was seven. When asked how the doll felt and what the doll thought, the man filled with tears. 'Sad,' he said in barely a whisper.

'What would you like to do to help him?' asked the facilitator.

'Give him a hug.'

'OK, go ahead,' she said.

For a long time there was silence in the training room as the trainee hugged this tiny doll. It was a very moving moment for most people in the room.

The facilitator waited several minutes until the trainee seemed to relax a bit. 'Are you ready to stop?' she asked.

'Yes,' he replied. 'Thank you.'

As with a child in therapy there was no need to process or discuss what had taken place. The trainee had dealt with what needed dealing with and he was ready to move on.

Matryoshkas and permissions

Matryoshkas and Permissions is an activity taken from our book *Matryoshkas in Therapy.* It can help children and young people to claim for themselves in the here and now permissions that they have not yet received in life. Psychotherapists Bob and Mary Goulding identified 12 types of negative decisions made in early childhood that they named 'injunctions' (Goulding & Goulding, 1976). Some of these 'Don't' messages are passed on to each of us, usually nonverbally, by parents and other significant adults.

Each injunction has an opposite known as a permission. 'Don't' messages are all-embracing with no way out, while permissions are usually preceded by 'It's OK to', giving the person a choice. So, it's OK to:

- *Exist.*
- *Be yourself.*
- *Be a child.*
- *Grow up.*
- *Make it.*
- *Be important.*
- *Be close.*
- *Belong.*
- *Be well.*
- *Be sane.*
- *Think.*
- *Feel.*

Here is a suggested way of using permissions with the matryoshkas when the client is old enough to read:

215

Open up the Russian dolls and spread them out on the table. Have a look at the list and choose a permission for each of the dolls.

Now, hold each Russian doll in turn. What is that permission likely to look like, sound like and feel like? Describe the doll as if they already had that permission.

Celebrate the success of the doll in accepting that permission before moving on to the next one.

Therapeutic purpose: Helping young clients to find positive ways forward to counteract any negatives they have had in their lives so far.

23
Recommended reading

Here is a list of recommended reading for counsellors wanting to adapt their therapeutic skills to working with children, young people and families. They are strongly advised to read at least one or two of these books before starting to work with clients under the age of 16.

Ariel, Shlomo (2002). *Children's Imaginative Play: A visit to wonderland.* Westport, CT: Greenwood Publishing Group.

Baxter, Kate, et al (1994). *Fundamental Activities Handbook.* Nottingham: Fundamental Activities.

Brandes, Donna, & Phillips, Howard (1979). *Gamesters' Handbook: 140 games for teachers and group leaders.* London: Hutchinson. (Original work published 1977.)

Drost, Joost, & Bailey, Sydney (2017). *Therapeutic Groupwork with Children.* Bicester: Speechmark. (Original publication 2001.)

Gladwell, Malcolm (2006). *Blink: The power of thinking without thinking.* London: Penguin.

Jennings, Sue (2017). *Creative Drama in Groupwork.* Abingdon, Oxfordshire: Routledge.

Kranowitcz, Carol Stock (2005). *The Out-of-Sync Child: Recognising and coping with Sensory Process Disorder.* London: Penguin/Skylight Press. (Original work published 1998.)

Kranowitz, Carol Stock (2006). *The Out-of-Sync Child Has Fun: Activities for kids with sensory processing disorder.* New York: Perigee. (Original publication 2003.)

Leben, Norma (1993-1999*). Directive Group Play Therapy: 60 structured games for the treatment of ADHD, low self-esteem and traumatised children.* Pflugerville, Texas: Morning Glory Treatment Centre for Children.

McMahon, Linnet (1992). *The Handbook of Play Therapy.* London: Routledge.

Stern, Daniel (2000). *Interpersonal World of the Infant: A view from psychoanalysis and developmental psychology.* New York: Basic Books. (Original publication 1985.)

Stewart, Ian, & Joines, Vann (1987). *TA Today: A new introduction to Transactional Analysis.* Nottingham: Lifespace Publishing.

Tudor, Keith (2008). *The Adult is Parent to the Child: Transactional analysis with children and young people.* Lyme Regis, Dorset: Russell House Publishing.

Whitehouse, Éliane, & Pudney, Warwick (1998). *A Volcano in My Tummy: Helping children to handle anger.* Gabriola Island, British Columbia: New Society Publishers.

Wilson, Kate, & Ryan, Virginia (2005). *Play Therapy: A nondirective approach for children and adolescents,* Kate Wilson & Virginia Ryan, London: Baillière Tindall. (Original work published 1992.)

24
Group therapy with children and young people

Introduction

Here are some of the first questions counsellors might ask about children's and young person's therapy groups:

- *Why have therapy groups at all?*
- *Why not just do individual work?*
- *Is it just so that I can see more children?*
- *Is it because children are in groups at school and they are used to that approach?*

Positive reasons for forming a therapy group with children or young people include:

- *Working with others gives them confidence to explore changes in their lives.*
- *Helping each other as a team.*
- *Working with other children rather than only with an adult.*
- *Having fun together.*
- *Experiencing less pressure because the focus isn't just on one person.*

Our strong recommendation in running a children's therapy group is to have two counsellors or one counsellor and an adult helper who has some knowledge of working with children. A group of four to eight clients is ideal. Any more than eight could be unmanageable and less helpful to the group members.

Children and young people of various ages work well together in a group, though it is probably best to have separate groups for primary and secondary age young clients.

An ideal length of a group is six sessions, with no new clients joining part way through. Groups work well as directive ones – the therapist sets the programme.

Specialist groups can often work well. We have had successful specialist groups involving children who have been abused, those with anger issues and those who have a diagnosis on the autistic spectrum.

Setting up the group

Now let's look at the kind of young clients to have in a group. A counsellor could, of course, accept people at random and hope for the best. Another way is to select the group members so that they can form an effective group. It is essential to avoid mixing people with trauma with those who have issues around hyperactivity. They simply don't mix. When young clients are referred for therapy, it is important to find out the type of person each one is before slotting them into the next available group.

Types of group member include:

■ *Clown.*
■ *Invisible man.*
■ *Attention seeker.*
■ *Dominator.*
■ *Reluctant member.*
■ *Rescuer.*
■ *Manipulator.*
■ *Little Professor.*

The other very important element is that any group of children/young people or family needs a structure. Once the structure is in place, the counsellor can then fit the actual activities for each weekly session. Here is a structure we have used together in running our younger children's groups:

1. *Check-in.*
2. *Game.*
3. *Quiet activity.*
4. *Worksheet.*
5. *Lively moving activity.*
6. *Quieter moving activity.*
7. *Check-out.*

Checking in and checking out

At the beginning and end of each group session it is useful to introduce the group to a different fun activity for a check-in and a check-out. Below are some ideas for this using words that the therapist can use:

Name and food
We'll now introduce ourselves to each other. What I want you to do is say your name and what food you like that starts with the first letter of your name. So, my name is Christine and I like cucumber.

__Once everyone has spoken:__ Now, who can go around the group and say what food each person likes?

Rainstick
We are going to use a rainstick as a way of checking out [or checking in]. Use it in a way that shows how you are feeling now, adding some words if you would like.

Small objects
In front of us there are a number of small objects. In a moment please choose one of them. I would like you to do this intuitively. In other words, let the object choose you. If two people want the same object then use your intuition a second time! Once you have the object, hold it in your hand and wait for the next instruction.

When everyone is ready: Now that you have your object I would like us to go around and introduce ourselves. Say your name and a little about yourself. Then say how you think the object you chose speaks about you.

Spider's web
We're going to pass this ball of wool around the circle making a spider's web pattern with it. We all need to hold a part of the wool in our hand. Someone starts by holding the wool and making a connection with another person in the group by throwing or passing the ball of wool. That person then introduces themselves, holds a piece of the wool and passes it on. This continues with everyone having two or three turns until we have made a web of connections.

No words
In turn I would like you to introduce yourself to the group without using words. You can use things you have brought with you or anything here in the room. See how much you can convey about yourself without words. Before we start you have a couple of minutes to plan how you'll communicate with the rest of us.

Movement
We'll now introduce ourselves to each other. In a minute I'll invite us all to stand in a circle. Then each group member in turn steps forward, gives their name and at the same time makes a clear gesture or movement of their choice. We all then echo the name and movement and the person repeats both in response to the group. The group then echoes the name and movement a second time. When everyone has introduced themselves we'll go round again saying the name and doing the same movement, this time keeping in a rhythm if we can.

Feelings check-out

At the end of a session: In turns say how you are feeling and one positive idea you can take away from this session.

Sandtray object

At the end of a session: Choose a sandtray object one at a time to help you say goodbye. Say one thing that has helped you, then place the object in this sandtray in relationship to the other objects there.

Puppet

Choose a puppet and in turns get your puppet in their voice to say one thing the puppet has noticed that you learned from today [or that you hope to learn today] that can help you in your life.

Therapeutic purpose: These and other check-ins and check-outs bring the group together as a team, enabling them to have fun and also learn a little more about themselves. They are without doubt one of the most important – even vital – parts of any therapeutic group with children and young people.

The school-based therapy group consisted of eight very quiet boys and girls who had been chosen by their teachers because of their low confidence and poor socialising skills. They came from different parts of the school and ranged in age from seven to 11.

The two therapists thought of the group as 'The Mice'. For the first couple of sessions the children hardly spoke at all. The few words they each spoke were barely audible even in the quiet of the closed school library. When they took part in the various activities they did so hesitantly at first.

As each session unfolded they became more involved. The older children started to encourage and support the younger ones. Soon they were functioning well as a group, almost as if they were a team.

Particularly noticeable was that their talking became louder as each session progressed. They also began to laugh instead of just smiling. A breakthrough happened when they were given a balloon each and asked to make as many noises with their balloon as they could. They came up with many different sounds as they took turns around the group. By the end of the activity the whole group was in fits of healthy, happy laughter.

The sixth and final session was marked by loud and incessant chatter. It was difficult for the therapists to get a word in edgeways. The eight 'Mice' had become as noisy as eight monkeys, although the therapists thought of them as powerful as Lions.

Later the eight children sent the therapists a thank-you card saying how helpful they had found the sessions. The headteacher, too, wrote to say how helpful the therapy had been for the children.

Below are some activities that can be used with groups of children (and, if appropriate, with individual families). In between the activities are further thoughts and ideas about running a therapy group with children.

Favourite animal

Favourite Animal is a useful activity for a children's or young people's group to explore their relationship with each other. Here is a suggested way of instructing the children:

Find an empty part of the room and lie down or crouch down on the floor with your eyes closed. It's been a long night and you've been deeply asleep. Think for a moment about your favourite animal. [PAUSE] Is it big or small? Furry, feathery, scaly? Is it strong or friendly? [PAUSE]

Now slowly wake up as your favourite animal. [PAUSE] You may need to adjust your position to become the animal. Stretch, then begin to move around as the animal. Maybe eating and drinking. [PAUSE]

Move around the room and think about the animal you have become. Is it friendly or angry? [PAUSE] Fast? Soft? Safe? [PAUSE] Exciting? [PAUSE] What's the best thing it can do?

How does your animal feel towards the other animals in the room? [PAUSE]

OK, now stop being your animal, turn once round and become the person you are. What was it like being the animal? How did you react to the other animals in the room?

Therapeutic purpose: Self-awareness, creativity, building confidence, relating to others.

Toilet paper game

The Toilet Paper Game is a surprising and usually fun activity for therapy groups. The leader holds up a toilet roll and says something like:

*Here is something very familiar. Please tear off as much as you would **like** (not what you **need**), tear it into sections and put it on one knee.*

Once everyone has done this, the therapist springs the surprise:

*Now, to move each piece of paper from one knee to the other I would like you to say one positive thing about yourself. This is about things **you** say about yourself, not what **others** say about you. Saying what you like doesn't count. Then the next person says something positive about themselves and moves one piece of paper. We continue until everyone is finished.*

For this activity it is helpful if the adults in the room take part as well as the children and young people. This will encourage the children to overcome any reticence to speak out. Often children who have come for counselling will find saying positive things about themselves extremely difficult. The therapist can prompt them and can invite other children in the group who know the person to do the same. It is worth persisting until every piece of paper has been moved.

Therapeutic purpose: To help children acknowledge their positives, to build self-esteem, to develop socialising skills, to discover areas in their lives where they are happy about themselves.

Functions of groups

Groups using an exercise such as *Favourite Animal* enable children to interact and act out some of their emotional problems in front of the therapist. The children's issues become noticed and important. This makes it easier to work with and understand some of these difficulties.

Children's and young people's groups are also a focus for empathy, belonging, fun and healing. If organised well they are also nonthreatening. The internal reaction is that the children learn to value themselves and relate to others of different ages and abilities.

Opposite sides of the room

In *Opposite Side of the Room* the children or adolescents learn to do some drama as they move from one side of the room to the other.

The therapist calls out two opposite situations. The clients start on one side of the room acting out the situation. Then, when the therapist gives the request, they walk from that side to the other side changing from one situation to the other.

The therapist could say something like: 'On this side of the room it is . . . and on this side of the room it is . . .'

Here are some opposite situations to use, though the therapist will no doubt think of others:

stormy	calm
raining	dry
slippery footpath	firm footpath
deep mud	solid ground
snowing	sunny
winter	summer
hot	cold
out of breath	relaxed

Therapeutic purpose: Enabling children and young people to act, finding different ways to express themselves, learning to empathise in different situations, building confidence.

Make-a-pizza massage

Make-a-Pizza Massage is a group activity that involves making an imaginary pizza on each other's backs. The group members need to have reached the stage where they are comfortable with each other. The group (including the counsellor if appropriate) stands in a circle close enough so that each person can reach the back of the person in front of them.

Then the counsellor invites some creative imagination involving the person's back. It is important to have rules about respect for the other person, including about being careful with their movements. Here are some proposed words:

First spread some flour on the surface. [PAUSE] Knead the dough. [PAUSE] Then smooth it out into a circle to make a base. Spread on the tomato paste. [PAUSE] Now for the toppings. First put some slices of ham on. [PAUSE] Dot the olives all over the pizza. [PAUSE] Sprinkle with corn. [PAUSE] Scatter mushrooms here and there. [PAUSE] Add slices of tomato. [PAUSE] Sprinkle on the cheese. [PAUSE] Put it in the oven. [PAUSE] It's ready. Take it out of the oven. [PAUSE] Slice it. [PAUSE] Now eat it. [PAUSE]

Therapeutic purpose: Safe and appropriate physical contact, respect for other people, self-acceptance, fun.

Group structure and dynamics

There are several ways of understanding the structure and dynamics of the group. Psychiatrist Eric Berne (Berne, 1966) talked about time structuring and this helps to see the stages of the children's therapy group:

Withdrawal – during this stage the person avoids the risk of rejection by others.
Ritual – adapting to the cultural and expected norms.
Pastimes – talking *about* something but not engaging in action concerning it.
Activities – directing energy towards some material outcome.
Games – exchanging a sequence of transactions leading to bad feelings.
Intimacy/closeness – no secret messages, feelings expressed to finish stage.

A well-known way of understanding how a group develops is by Bruce Tuckman (1965). He talked about the stages of:

Forming
Storming
Norming
Performing.
Mourning. (This final stage was added at a later date.)

This last stage of Mourning is very important in children's and young people's groups. Norma Leben (2000) talks about the importance of therapeutic terminations with groups, suggesting that the group holds a special ceremony for the leaving group member. The individual and the rest of the group share their feelings and decide whether future contact is made and how that will be done.

Berne (1973/1963) also developed four stages for a group. He called these *imagoes* and the word refers to the way a group member *imagines* the rest of the group. Interestingly, Berne, too, left out the final stage, which has been termed by others as 'Clarified'. Napper & Newton (2000) have put together Berne's imagoes and Tuckman's stages to form the following sequence:

Imagine – forming
There's me, the leader and all these others.

Meet – storming
Conflict and rebellion.

Angling – norming
Cohesion of the group, jostling to find a place.

Get on – performing
Move to calling it 'my group'. Recognises others. Gives and gets strokes.

Clarified – mourning
Ending – a vital stage for children's groups.

Music machine

Music Machine is a noisy yet fun activity that can involve the whole group.

The first person in the group stands up and makes a noise, then an action like a machine. This is kept up throughout the activity. Then the next person stands up, makes a different noise, and a different action like a machine. The next person continues with a different noise and action.

Eventually the whole group (including hopefully the counsellor) will form a music machine.

Therapeutic purpose: Cooperation and coordination, building confidence, finding joy again.

I am a shoe

The exercise *I Am a Shoe* is a useful one for a quiet point in one week's programme. Here is a form of words:

I would like you to sit quietly and look around the room. Notice an object and imagine what it would be like to be that object. Now let's go around and introduce ourselves as those objects. Give three qualities the object has. For example, I am a shoe, I am warm, soft and comfortable.

After everyone has spoken:

Now I want you to do exactly the same, this time using your name and saying the three qualities you named for the object.

For example: *I am Bill, I am warm, soft and comfortable.*

After everyone has had a turn, it is useful to discuss what the activity was like for people within the group.

Therapeutic purpose: Enables children and young people to become self-aware and provides a means of self-disclosure. Helps to build the young client's self-esteem. Above all, it provides plenty of fun.

Embodiment, Projection, Role

When young clients engage in group activities such as *Opposite Sides of the Room, Music Machine* and *I Am a Shoe,* they are taking part in a form of drama.
Dramatherapist Dr Sue Jennings has identified three stages in playing and drama that are often replayed in

therapy groups: Embodiment, Projection and Role (Jennings, 2017). This drama model can be linked with the first three stages of child development as presented by Pam Levin-Landheer (1982):

Embodiment (Being) is the stage where the child's early experiences are expressed through body movement and the senses. The child needs to explore what they can do with their body and feel confident about moving around. The older child returning to this stage may need to explore spatial awareness, touch and eye contact.

Projection (Doing) is a stage reached usually when a child first starts holding their transitional object, such as a teddy or blanket. The child explores the world beyond their body. The older child revisiting projection may enjoy working with clay, finger paint and drawing materials.

Role (Thinking) is the final stage, where the child uses objects to tell stories, then becomes characters within stories. The small child will want to dress up every day. Puppets are ideal at this stage for children revisiting Role. So too are group dramas, body movement and gestures. Children will enjoy mimicking different sounds and being somebody else.

Parachute names

A play parachute makes a useful tool for many different group activities. This one is called *Parachute Names.*

Everyone – including the therapist – stands in a circle holding a piece of the play parachute. Then, on the count of three, they lift it up in the air, hold it for a second, then bring it down again. A second stage is to lift up the parachute and walk three steps in, hold for a couple of seconds and then walk back again.

The therapist then puts a lightweight ball in the middle of the parachute and invites the group to use their cooperative skills to pass this to people without touching the ball.

When the ball reaches someone, they take it in their hand, say their name and a bit about themselves, then throw the ball back into the middle. The activity is kept going until everyone has had a turn.

Play parachutes come in various sizes. The therapist chooses one according to their group size. There are many other therapeutic activities that can be done with a parachute to help children and young people with their emotional needs.

Therapeutic purpose: Cooperation, teambuilding, increasing confidence, developing hand-eye coordination.

Abandon ship

Abandon Ship is another exercise in cooperation and teambuilding. The therapist invites the children or young people to imagine that they are going on a journey in a small boat and it suddenly becomes stormy. The boat hits the rocks and is breaking up. They have just 15 minutes before the boat sinks.

Nearby is a small island that they can swim to. No one else lives there. They can take one bag of tinned food and only one thing from the following list:

Bucket
Rope
Radio
Football
Spade
Suntan cream
Tyre
Torch
Lighter
Spoon

Umbrella
Magnifying glass
Compass
Map
Spoon
Bottle

Each group member spends time on their own deciding what item they want to take with them. Then together in the group they decide what are the four most important of those items they want to take to the island and why they need them. They have to discuss with each other in order to make the decision.

After the group has decided on their four items, the therapist says to them:

Now you've selected your four items and arrived safely on the island, I've got some questions for you:

What will you use to collect drinking water?
How will you protect yourself from bad weather?
What can you do if wild animals attack you?
How are you going to open the tins in the bag you've collected?
How are you going to cook your food?
How will you contact people to tell them you are on the island?
A few months have gone by and the tins are finished. How will you get food?
A few years have gone by and the message you sent didn't get through. How will you escape?
Did you take the right items from the list?

Therapeutic purpose: This activity is about learning to negotiate, developing and building confidence, self-care, effective communication, team-building.

Magic wand

This activity involves using a magic wand that is passed around the group. It can be any kind of stick such as a chopstick.

Everyone has a turn at being the leader. The person who is the leader whispers to someone in the group what (polite) action they want them to do. It can be anything from jumping up and down to doing a star jump. Then the leader waves the magic wand and the person performs it.

The rest of the group has to guess what exactly was the request. Then the next person takes the magic wand and whispers to someone else. This is kept going until everyone has had a turn.

Therapeutic purpose: Promoting empowerment, building self-esteem, enhancing communication skills, promoting body awareness, refining motor coordination, developing a keen sense of observation.

Group programme

When a counsellor works with young clients in a group it is important that the programme is consistent from one week to another. Children (and adults) feel comfortable with routine. Planning it that way ensures that the group always has the same elements in each session.

It could be helpful to the parents, teachers and possibly social workers involved with the children and young people coming for therapy to be given the outline programme, leaving out the details if the counsellor thinks that would be best.

One way of developing a suitable group programme is based on Pam Levin's Cycles of Development (Levin-Landheer, 1975/1988):

Being   Warm-up, opener, ice breaker.

Doing   Focusing, group activities.

Thinking   Input, worksheet.

Identity   Application, how the activity relates to life.

Skills/structure   Practice, more group activity.

Integration   Consolidation and check-out.

25
Talking business

For 23 years we ran our therapy with adults, children and families as a business rather than a sideline. Apart from two children's therapy groups as part of our own training, we always charged for our services. Even when we lived and worked in Romania for four years we ensured that all therapy was paid for, based on local rates.

Of course, some people are committed to working therapeutically with children on a voluntary or part-time basis. There isn't a problem with that. It's just that in this chapter we want to share some of our experiences and learning while earning during the 23-year-period.

How much to charge

Children and young people usually have a reduction in the cost of most things: entry to events, bus and train fares. There is therefore a tendency for parents and carers to expect half price or less for counselling their children or young people.

Over the years we took a different view. Counselling children is much more challenging than working with over 16s. It is generally harder work than working with adults and is more draining emotionally for the practitioner.

A counsellor is expected to work for a maximum of 20 sessions a week. Roger found that he could only manage 15 sessions before becoming emotionally drained. This means that the therapist will need to charge enough for those 15 or 20 sessions to pay the bills. Remember that there is also a need to spend a lot of money on supervision, insurance, professional memberships, ongoing training and possibly personal therapy.

At the time of publishing this book a fee of £50 to £60 per session was not an unreasonable amount to charge. Anything less is probably a discounted rate.

When things are quiet

In addition to providing counselling, it is important to plan for when there aren't enough clients to bring in sufficient money.

It usually takes a couple of years to build up sufficient interest in parents bringing their children or young people for counselling. This means that during most of those couple of years the counsellor will need to earn money elsewhere.

Unless they are on a fixed salary, the counsellor will need to supplement their income. Hobbies, interests and previous job experiences could be considered in planning to earn extra money. In our case we have, at different stages, earned extra money from writing and editing, bookkeeping, selling online, administering counselling in general practice for a year and counselling in jobcentres for about 10 years, providing supervision and offering training courses in counselling subjects.

It is important to use some lateral thinking in order to choose the best forms of earning money that won't reduce the time available for clients, when they emerge.

Tax and ways to save money

A counsellor earning more than about £1000 per year is required to register with the UK tax office and fill in an annual tax return. For a counsellor working with children, young people and families there are a number of ways to save money through claiming legitimate expenses for the business.

These could cover a proportion of car expenses – including car depreciation – telephone costs and household expenses. Other items include stationery, publicity and furniture for the therapy room.

In all cases it is important to keep every possible receipt, even handwritten ones.

Equipping the therapy room with play items can involve considerable tax savings. When we were setting up, buying small items from a charity or other secondhand shop took up a large proportion of our expenses. Each time we purchased something we wrote on the receipt what the item was and the purpose it would be used for. Our receipts, strange as they must have seemed, were never questioned.

The annual tax return is designed so that it can be completed by the person concerned. We did our own bookkeeping, using a simple money program on the computer. However, we used a professional accountant to complete our books and make the tax return. The few hundreds of pounds we spent on this each year was more than made up by the legitimate savings our accountant made for us.

26
Therapy outdoors

Introduction

Working outdoors with groups of child or adolescent clients can, in our experience, be enjoyable, challenging and actually speed up the process of therapeutic change. It gives plenty of space for clients to work through their emotional issues without the restriction of the therapy room.

Therapy outdoors can take place in forests, hills and mountains. It can also be used successfully in a field or a park. Each different setting will require adapting the activities to suit the conditions, and the age and physical fitness of the children or young people.

There are a number of safety issues to take into account when working outdoors. First, it is almost never acceptable for an adult counsellor to be alone in fields, hills or woods with an individual young client. It is a true saying in this case that there is safety in numbers. The key to safeguarding in this case is working in a group, preferably with a second adult.

It is vital that the parent or carer of each child taking part signs an agreement to the proposed therapy outdoors. It might also be worth suggesting to parents/carers that they take out personal insurance for their child. This usually covers mishaps that are caused by the child or young person rather than the therapist.

It is important to ensure that children/young people are suitably dressed for therapy outdoors. This might include a hat and sunscreen or a jumper and a good waterproof jacket as well as strong shoes/trainers/boots.

Another issue to consider is confidentiality. In the therapy room the usual contract with people under the age of 16 is something like:

This is confidential unless you are going to hurt yourself, hurt someone else or someone is hurting you.

The same three elements apply outdoors. The main difference is that in the outdoors it is possible to be near other people during the therapy. A useful way to handle this is to include in the confidentiality contract words similar to the following, depending on the young client's age and understanding:

If someone comes within hearing distance, any conversation is stopped and, if necessary, a cheerful Hello is given. Then the conversation can start again once the person is out of hearing range.

This will probably cover emotional safety. Physical safety is also vital. How will the counsellor ensure safety of their clients? It is always best to have an extra person (not necessarily a counsellor) whose main duty is to keep a close eye on any serious hazards the clients may face. If the activities involve adventure-type activities, the counsellor would be well advised in advance to attend a training course in outdoor activities and/or the second adult is skilled or qualified in the activities planned.

The issue of professional indemnity insurance also needs considering. This usually covers incidents related to the counsellor. Some well-known companies that insure counsellors refuse to insure anything that is therapeutic taking place outside the therapy room. Others willingly include such activities as part of their policy. It is important for the counsellor to check with their current insurance company and switch to another provider if necessary.

Further information on this exciting aspect of therapy is available in our book *Therapeutic Adventure: 64 activities for therapy outdoors* (Day & Day, 2008/2015).

Crowd surfing in nature

Crowd Surfing in Nature involves a group of people raising one of its members above their heads in a horizontal position facing upwards, and then carrying the person across a field or through a clearing in the forest.

The counsellor chooses a spot that is relatively free of obstructions that could trip people over. It is essential that the group has already gelled together because this exercise involves considerable trust. The person who is to be carried lies back into the arms of the team. It is best for the person to fold arms, relax and keep eyes closed. The team then carefully lift the person (the distributed weight makes this fairly easy) and walk across the field with them. When the team reach the other side of the field, they carefully lower the person to the ground.

The activity continues until everyone who wants to has had a turn. Some of the clients may want more than one turn.

Therapeutic purpose: Trust, concentration and group development. It is also plenty of fun. It may be a useful experience for the therapist and the participants if *the therapist* has a turn at becoming the person being carried.

Blind walk

This exercise involves one person going on a walk in the great outdoors (hills, forest, park) with the rest of the group following. The difference with *Blind Walk* is that everyone except the person in front is blindfolded for the whole walk.

Before starting the walk the therapist gets the clients to decide how those who are blindfolded will know where to go. They could follow verbal signals, hold hands or hold waists. The participants are given the choice.

The therapist might take the lead, or they might get a client to take the lead. Bear in mind that if one participant leads, many of the others will want a turn, too.

A variation could be one person leading while the therapist joins the rest of the participants wearing a blindfold. Bear in mind that, unless the therapist has another assistant with them, there is a slight risk if they as well as most of the clients are blindfolded.

This is an activity that warrants discussion afterwards to see how people felt and what they thought about taking part. Also, what had they learned from this activity?

Therapeutic purpose: To facilitate teamwork and trust. This activity gives the participants a choice in how communication is achieved. It also encourages taking initiative and building confidence.

The 12-year-old client was part of a therapy group working outdoors, facilitated by two counsellors.

In a trust activity she fell back with her arms folded and her eyes closed, believing that the rest of the group would catch her, lift her horizontally on to her back and carry her along. She bent backwards to touch the ground and held her position as blindfolded group members had to find their way through a human obstacle course that she had helped to create.

In the woods she sat on the ground partly hidden by a bush as she and the whole group engaged in 15 minutes on their own. She enjoyed time perhaps to reflect, meditate or pray, while waiting for the therapist's whistle to blow, ending the activity.

The client created a woodland 'sandtray' by clearing a small area and bordering it with sticks. Then she used natural objects to make a scene in the area she had cleared. When the therapists asked her about her creation she just pointed as tears flowed down her face.

Although the counsellors never knew exactly what she had achieved in the therapy outdoors, it was obvious that this client had been deeply moved by the activities.

Appendix A

Safeguarding policy

Introduction to the organisation

[Name of organisation] is a private organisation providing counselling for adults and children, individually and in groups.

Introduction to the safeguarding policy

Although [name of organisation] is privately run, it works with other counselling organisations and training establishments. Its safeguarding policy therefore takes account of its external as well as its in-house work. Its policy is outlined below. This is in the process of development, and changes will be notified on its website [www.nameoforganisation.com] and elsewhere as they become available. A full review of the policy will be made by [a date in three years' time].

Standard 1: Policy

This policy is based on the United Nations Convention on the Rights of Children, under which protection of children (up the age of 18) from abuse and exploitation is paramount.

[Name of organisation] is deeply committed to protecting children it works with. It seeks to protect them from all forms of abuse, including sexual, physical and emotional abuse. It will also seek wherever possible to protect children from neglect, abandonment and exploitation. Children need protecting where they live (family or care home) as well as from any dangers posed at school, in the playground or elsewhere outside.

[Name of organisation] recognises that when child abuse is suspected, children often experience unintentional abuse by being interviewed by social services or the police, or even separated from family members or placed in care. It will seek wherever possible to put the child's needs first in such situations by being involved as much as it can with the statutory organisations.

With this in mind, [name of organisation] will seek to establish a good working relationship with local social services children's teams and police child protection/safeguarding departments.

Standard 2: Procedures and systems

Where abuse is suspected of or reported by a child in [name of organisation]'s programmes, the person with the concern will in the first instance discuss the matter with the organisation's Safeguarding Officer [name]. If the child is at immediate risk the officer with make a direct call to the children's team of the local social services department seeking to work with them on a professional-to-professional basis. In cases where there is no immediate risk of harm to the child, the officer may call a case conference or seek further specialist advice. The case conference would consist of all those involved in the welfare of the child. This may include parents, teachers, social workers and therapists. Further specialist advice may be sought from a specialist social work agency such as CCPAS (telephone: 0303 003 1111).

Where it is clear that the matter must be reported, the officer will contact the children's team and seek to work with them on a professional-to-professional basis. If it is likely that a crime has been committed, the police will be informed so that they can conduct an investigation. This will uphold the law and hopefully prevent further abuse.

All discussion of a child considered at risk will be written down with time and date, and notes kept in a secure, locked cabinet. Confidentiality to protect the child's rights will be respected unless the child's safety is at risk. Everyone involved in discussion about a suspected incident of child abuse will agree to these levels of confidentiality.

[Name of organisation] will aim to provide appropriate therapy for the child and for others concerned. If the child is expected later to be called as a witness, the therapy will be conducted within the guidelines of the Crown Prosecution Service on provision of therapy for child witnesses:

www.cps.gov.uk/publications/prosecution/therapychild.html

In such cases any therapy avoids direct discussion of details of the abuse until after the case has been heard in court.

Complaints about people working for or associated with [name of organisation] should be addressed to the designated Safeguarding Officer [name] (mobile telephone xxxxx xxx xxx). Should the complaint need to be made about [name of Safeguarding Officer] or any member of their family the emergency designated Safeguarding Officer is [person outside the organisation], a qualified counsellor (mobile telephone xxxx xxx xxx).

Standard 3: Prevention

[Name of organisation] requires anyone wanting to work for them in whatever capacity to undertake a Disclosure and Barring Service (DBS) enhanced check:

https://www.gov.uk/disclosure-barring-service-check/overview

If the check shows convictions that are likely to put children at risk, [name of organisation] reserves the right to refuse the services of the person, whether the services are voluntary or not. In addition, each person will need to provide at least two written character references about them from trustworthy people.

If abuse is later suspected by an associate, the person concerned will be suspended while a full investigation is conducted by [name of organisation], the local social services and/or the police. If the abuse is confirmed, the person will be removed from the books of [name of organisation] and recommended to undergo intensive therapy. He or she will be deemed a danger to children and steps may be taken to warn other groups of the person's danger to children.

Standard 4: Codes of practice and behaviour

[Name of organisation]'s therapeutic work is undertaken in a way that ensures safe, ethical practice. The therapist makes sure that someone else is present in the building where the work is being done. In some cases the person (such as a parent or carer) is present in the room. In other cases, the person is outside the room. This could be a parent waiting for their child, a fellow therapist or even someone else working or living in the building. If that person is aware that therapy is going on, they can be attuned to any difficulties and available in case of problems.

Almost all therapy takes place in a room with the door shut. This is standard practice for most therapists. There are instances, however, when leaving the door slightly ajar can be therapeutically justified, even if it means compromising confidentiality by risking someone overhearing what is happening. The child with extreme anxiety or claustrophobia is a case in point. So too is the child who has been subjected to sexual abuse behind a closed door, such as a bedroom or bathroom. In these instances, not only does the client feel safe but the therapist can feel less vulnerable.

Child clients are generally expected to stay in the room throughout the session. There are a few exceptions to this rule. These include children who have experienced being locked in their bedroom as a punishment and those who have not been allowed out of a room until they have engaged in a sexual activity with an abuser. In these rare instances the therapist gives the child permission to leave the room as often as she/he needs to.

[Name of organisation]'s therapists will sometimes video or audio-record the session, with the agreement of the parent/carer and the child concerned. The video or audio recording is for note-taking and training purposes only and is kept in a locked cabinet and not on any computer. It is available for loan to the parent/carer only with the clear agreement of the child and the therapist. On occasion therapists may decide to video sessions where it is likely that the client will become manipulative and make false allegations.

Since most issues with children impact on and are affected by the system (family, school, etc), it is sometimes appropriate to involve the parent/carer or brothers and sisters in some or all of the sessions. Having another person present, providing it is therapeutically justified, is a major contribution towards safe, ethical practice. It is especially important with the child who is either flirtatious or is known to be acting out sexually.

In its training and supervision work, [name of organisation] will help trainees and supervisees to identify any potential safeguarding issues in their work. It is for the trainee/supervisee to take forward any safeguarding measures needed, with support from [name of organisation].

Children often need physical contact. With this in mind [name of organisation] has developed a Safe Touch policy as part of its safeguarding. This is now widely used by other organisations. There are five principles:

1. Always have other people in sight
The therapist avoids being on their own with a child of any age.

2. Ensure that the child wants the physical contact being offered

Where possible make eye contact with the child and indicate with gestures or verbally what is proposed, waiting for the child's clear agreement. If the therapist believes a child may have been abused, it is important to avoid physical contact until the child has learned the difference between 'good' touching and 'bad' touching. This may take many sessions to build up the trust needed.

3. Touch in appropriate areas only

Consciously avoid touching the child in areas of the body that would be covered by a swimming costume. Touching the child's leg above the knee is also generally not acceptable.

4. Be cautious about having a child on your lap

Men especially are strongly advised to avoid children sitting on their laps. In exceptional circumstances they may let a small child sit on the knee end of their lap.

5. Avoid face-to-face hugging of a girl who has begun to develop

This is especially important with men. Instead of a face-to-face hug, try an arm on the shoulder 'sideways hug'. This satisfies the older girl's need for closeness and avoids inappropriate physical contact.

Special precautions are required when working with children who have a disability because of the increased risk of physical abuse or sexual exploitation. Only in very exceptional circumstances will an associate of [name of organisation] be alone with a disabled child. Helping the child change clothes or to go to the toilet must always be done with the door open and, if at all possible, in the presence of another adult.

[Name of organisation]'s child-to-child policy includes addressing any public or age-inappropriate sexualised behaviour with another child, whether or not the two children are of the same age. While such behaviour may provide useful therapeutic clues to the child's possible problematic background, it is essential that such behaviour is addressed to avoid any abuse arising as a result.

Children will be encouraged strongly to respect each other at all times. This includes avoiding any physical or verbal aggression towards another child because of the child's own anger problems. Bullying or harassment of any sort will also not be tolerated.

Standard 5: Implementation in different cultural contexts

[Name of organisation] works mainly in Great Britain and Northern Ireland. Its safeguarding policy applies in all its work, taking account of the different cultures it works with. Aspects of the safeguarding policy may need to be adjusted when considering different cultures.

Standard 6: Equality

From its inception, [name of organisation] has been deeply committed to equality for children and adults it is involved with, regardless of culture, language, religious adherence, age, gender, level of ability/disability, socio-economic group or sexual preference. In all its training programmes it promotes equality and protection for children.

Standard 7: Communication and keeping notes

[Name of organisation] publishes its safeguarding policy on its website www.xxx.com as well as in workshops on working therapeutically with children.

Wherever possible, children's views on protecting themselves will be heard and included within the policy.

From time to time photographs of children's work will be taken and may be used anonymously by [name of organisation] on websites or in emails. [Name of organisation] will seek to ensure that the child does not appear in any picture. It will also ensure that other identifying features contained in any work will be removed. Where appropriate, permission from the parent/carer of the child concerned will be obtained in advance of the use of such photographs. Part of this permission is to inform the parent/carer exactly how the picture will be used, including any captions or digital change proposed.

Part of safeguarding includes confidentiality in the therapy room unless the child client is likely to harm self, harm others or be harmed by another person. Such confidentiality extends to note-keeping. [Name of organisation] ensures that all confidential notes, whether handwritten, typed and printed or held in a computer do not contain details about the client that could identify them. A coding system is used, and details of the code are stored separate from any computer or other recording device in a locked cabinet.

Standard 8: Education and training

[Name of organisation] provides training about safeguarding for its associates. This training is based on its own policy as well as including resources from experts elsewhere. The training will include how offenders operate – the cycle of abuse and 'grooming' of a potential victim, and 'sexting'.

Standard 9: Access to advice and support

[Name of organisation] is aware of the importance for children who have been or are being abused to have a way of getting help. It favours the model exemplified by ChildLine, where the child can speak on the telephone in confidence with a trained counsellor about what is concerning her or him (telephone 0800 1111). It also favours local initiatives where children who have been abused can seek advice and support in person, on-line or by telephone.

Standard 10: Implementation and monitoring

[Name of organisation] as a small organisation is able to monitor any incidents of noncompliance with its safeguarding policy and to take appropriate action quickly. Any such incidents will start with a strategy meeting to propose a way forward.

In the case of a complaint being made about a staff member or associate, [name of organisation]'s own supervision network will be involved as quickly as possible. This will include its professional supervisor [name and telephone number]. Again, the police and/or social services will be informed if appropriate.

Standard 11: Working with partners

[Name of organisation] seeks to work cooperatively with other organisations. Such partnerships will include [name of organisation] providing training, consultancy, supervision and therapy for professionals as well as for adults and children being helped by the organisation.

Where working with children or training in child therapy is involved, [name of organisation] expects such partnership organisations to have in place, or be in the process of developing, their own safeguarding policy and procedures. Such policy and procedures need to be consistent with the standards outlined in this document.

Safeguarding issues that arise as a result of working with partners will be referred back to the partner organisation by [name of organisation] for appropriate action.

Standard 12: On-line policy and procedures

[Name of organisation] is committed to ensuring electronic safety as part of its safeguarding policy. This includes the use of mobile telephones, laptops, netbooks, tablets and other electronic devices that may be developed in the future. It covers access to the internet and sending emails, messaging and text messages. It also includes social media sites such as Facebook, Instagram, Twitter and Snaphat. The policy covers personal use of computers as well as electronic communication as part of the organisation's work.

[Name of organisation]'s counsellors and other staff agree that they will not use [name of organisation]'s computer systems for illegal purposes or for storing unlawful text, images or sound. They will not delete search history from any of its devices. They will also ensure that in their private use of the internet they do not view or download images or videos that could be considered unlawful, particularly any such involving children.

[Name of organisation]'s counsellors are expected to monitor any on-line communications they make concerning children and young people. Reminders of appointments using text or other electronic means sent to people under 18 need to be copied to a parent or other responsible adult. All such messages must finish with the therapist's name. It is important to avoid the use of ambiguous abbreviations. For instance, 'lol' could mean 'laugh out loud' or 'lots of love'.

Counsellors and staff with [name of organisation] will avoid using social networking sites such as Facebook, Twitter, Instagram and Snapchat to communicate with clients under the age of 18. With the exception of family members, they will not add or accept people under 18 on to their private social media sites. They will also set their private social media accounts to the highest level of privacy and security. This will avoid clients and former clients having access to personal information.

[Name]
Safeguarding Officer
[Month and year of policy]

[Name of organisation]
[Address, telephone, email, website]

Appendix B

Equal opportunities policy

1. Statement of Intent

[Name of organisation]'s policy on equal opportunities is based on the UK Sex Discrimination Act 1975 and 1986, the Race Relations Act 1976, the Disabled Persons (Employment) Act 1944 and 1958, the Disabled Persons Act 1986, the Disability Discrimination Act 1996 and the Department of Employment Code of Practice.

1.1 [Name of organisation] recognises that discrimination exists within the wider community and has a serious effect on many of the organisations with which it is working. It therefore gives equal regard to people, including clients, regardless of their culture, language, religious practice, gender, socio-economic group, sexual preference or physical or mental ability.

1.2 [Name of organisation]'s equal opportunities policy seeks to give due regard to people of every culture, language, religious practice, gender, socio-economic group, sexual preference or physical or mental ability/disability.

1.3 [Name of organisation] will give equal opportunities and positive action for employment and subcontract work to suitably qualified people regardless of their race, religion, gender, sexual orientation or physical or mental ability. It will seek to investigate and take appropriate action where any form of discrimination exists within its own organisation or sphere of influence.

1.4 [Name of organisation] understands that people are not all the same and come from different backgrounds, in terms of culture, language, religious practice, gender, socio-economic group, sexual preference and ability/disability. All people are to be treated with the same high regard and respect.

1.5 [Name of organisation] realises that people with physical or mental disabilities have the same right to respect as anyone else. It endeavours to provide suitable facilities and a network of support and help to anyone with disabilities attending therapy or working in [name of organisation]. It will also strongly encourage its subcontractors to provide such support and help to any employees within their organisations who have disabilities. Any discrimination by its subcontractors that becomes known to [name of organisation] will be challenged and, if action is not taken, will lead to a termination of subcontract work.

2. Procedures Relating to Recruitment, Training and Promotion

2.1 [Name of organisation]'s recruitment procedures for both direct employment and subcontracting work are fair to ensure that applicants are considered on merit alone and not on the basis of their culture, language, religious practice, gender, socio-economic group, sexual preference or physical or mental ability. It encourages positive action towards people with disabilities in its recruitment policies and seeks to make reasonable adjustments for people with disabilities, taking into account the social model of disability.

2.2 Training in issues relating to equal opportunities will be required for all employees and subcontractors within [name of organisation]. It is a condition of service that such training is regularly updated.

2.3 Advertisements for employees and subcontractors, including direct mail, will emphasise the need for qualified personnel from ethnic minority backgrounds and language groups. Such advertisements will invite applications from suitably qualified people 'regardless of culture, language, religious practice, gender, socio-economic group, sexual preference or physical or mental ability'.

3. Conditions of Service

3.1 [Name of organisation]'s employees and subcontractors will use facilities suitable to carry out their work effectively. In the case of people with disabilities, efforts will be made to ensure easy access to the premises (for example, ramps) and attempts made to procure specialist equipment that may be needed by the subcontractor/employee in order to carry out the tasks required.

3.2 [Name of organisation] will ensure as far as is reasonably possible that all its employees and subcontractors are safe in the working environment and that they have means of escape or other emergency procedures should they be threatened with attack or sexually harassed.

4. Grievance and Disciplinary Procedures

4.1 Grievances concerning equal opportunities within [name of organisation] should be made in the first instance to one of [name of organisation]'s owners, [name 1] or [name 2]. A full investigation and report will be made within 28 days of the grievance being received.

4.2 In the case of complaints made about [name of organisation] employees or subcontractors, disciplinary measures will be taken against anyone using racist or sexist words or behaviour, or who engages in sexual harassment or who makes disparaging or demeaning remarks about a person's disability. Such measures will start with a warning and could end with dismissal and/or court action against the person concerned.

5. Publicity

5.1 [Name of organisation] will take suitable action to ensure that awareness of discrimination is translated into positive action in favour of groups under-represented within its organisation.

5.2 [Name of organisation]'s policy on equal opportunities is published and made available to all existing employees and subcontractors. It is also given to all new/prospective employees/subcontractors.

6 Review

6.1 [Name of organisation]'s equal opportunities policy will be reviewed every three years. The next review will be in September 2015.

[name]
Director
[Name of organisation]

[date]

Appendix C

Health and safety policy

1. Statement of Intent

[Name of organisation]'s policy on health and safety is based on the UK's Health and Safety at Work Act 1974 and the Management of Health and Safety at Work Regulations 1999.

1.1 [Name of organisation] undertakes, so far as is reasonably practical, to ensure the health, safety and welfare at work of all its employees and subcontractors as well as its clients, supervisees and trainees.

1.2 [Name of organisation] seeks to provide such information, instruction, training and supervision as is necessary to ensure the health and safety at work of its employees and subcontractors.

1.3 [Name of organisation] will ensure as far as possible that the place of work is safe and without risks to health, and it will provide and maintain means of access and exit from its premises that are safe and without risks to health.

1.4 [Name of organisation] will ensure that it provides and maintains a safe working environment for its employees and subcontractors and its clients and trainees that is safe, without risks to health and adequate as regards facilities and arrangements for their welfare at work. [Name of organisation] employees and subcontractors visiting private offices or public buildings to conduct their work will check before they begin work that fire exits are clear and marked and that any clients they see will feel as safe as is reasonably practical.

1.5 It is the duty of [name of organisation] employees and subcontractors to take care for the health and safety of themselves and others. Employees and subcontractors will ensure, so far as is reasonably practicable, that people not in their employment are not exposed to risk of health or safety.

2. Organisation

2.1 Under the UK Safety Representatives and Safety Committees Regulations 1977, safety representatives will be appointed to investigate potential hazards and complaints from employees or subcontractors concerning the health, safety and welfare of employees and subcontractors. These representatives will be expected to attend meetings of safety committees as and when required.

2.2 [Name of organisation]'s owner, [name of counsellor], will have the ultimate responsibility for the health and safety of [name of organisation]'s staff. The line of responsibility then moves down from direct employees to subcontractors.

3. Arrangements

3.1 Each therapist within [Name of organisation] will be responsible for their own health and safety as well as that of visiting clients under their care. This safety will take into account codes of practice drawn up by professional bodies such as [names of professional counselling/therapy organisations]. In order to protect the safety of themselves and others, all therapists will be expected to have up-to-date professional liability insurance which includes public liability, professional indemnity, product liability, and libel and slander insurances.

3.2 Elements of safety to consider include fire safety, noise control, physical safety, and adequate warmth and lighting. In addition, therapists must ensure their own safety in working with clients known or believed to be violent or engaged in inappropriate sexual behaviour. They are expected to familiarise themselves with any available panic buttons and they are also strongly advised to undergo training in self-defence, restraint or breakaway techniques.

3.3 Therapists in particular will ensure that they have a safe environment free from interruption in which to conduct their therapeutic work with clients. Special attention needs to be made to telephones and public address systems and to windows and see-through doors that are accessible to members of the public or other personnel.

3.4 [Name of organisation] will take note of other health and safety regulations in the following UK legislation and in other legislation that may from time to time be introduced:

Health and Safety Information for Employees Regulations 1989
Reporting of Injuries, Diseases and Dangerous Occurrences Regulations 1985
Health and Safety (Display Screen Equipment) Regulations 1992
Health and Safety (First Aid) Regulations 1981

4. Review

4.1 [Name of organisation]'s health and safety policy will be reviewed every three years. The next review will be in [month and year in five years' time].

[Name of counsellor]
Director
[Name of organisation]

[Month and year]

Roger & Christine Day

Appendix D

Suggested list of materials for therapy with children

This list of play objects for use in therapy with children and young people is comprehensive and is probably only needed if the counsellor is working full-time with young clients. Otherwise, items (secondhand preferred) can be added as needed.

Sandtray

■ One or two sandtrays large enough to contain a number of objects and small enough for the counsellor to watch the client's face and see out of the corner of their eye what is being placed. The sandtrays can be wooden or plastic. The bottom is always blue to represent water or sky.
■ Play sand to fill the sandtrays to about half their depth.
■ Toys and other objects suitable for use in the sand (see below).

Toys

■ Play people, including ones representing different ethnic backgrounds and forms of disability.
■ Farm animals.
■ Wild animals.
■ Assorted dinosaurs.
■ Selection of small cars, trucks, tractors, etc.
■ Small dolls, baby-doll bottles and real baby-bottles.
■ A few assorted soft-play balls and stress balls.
■ Large inflatable punchbag.

■ Assorted musical instruments (beaters, shakers, etc).
■ Bridges, tunnels etc (perhaps broken off other toys) for sandtray.
■ Small non-breakable mirror.
■ Water tray and water play items.
■ A few face masks (plain ones in different colours, with elastic thread attached).

Puppets

■ Small assorted hand and glove puppets (those with and without a moving mouth). Animal characters are preferred, such as tiger, crocodile, monkey, lion, bee, spider, ladybird, mouse, ant. A mixture of 'nice' characters (ladybird, monkey) and 'not-so-nice' characters (crocodile, tiger) is essential. Puppets can be obtained from educational suppliers or from:

www.puppetsbypost.com

Craft materials

These don't all have to be brand new. They will need regularly replenishing.

■ 2 pairs scissors.
■ 1 stapler plus staples.
■ Large selection of felt tip pens in assorted sizes (avoid permanent markers) as well as crayons, pencils and erasers, highlighters.
■ Jars of glitter, shapes, stars, coloured sand, sequins, etc.
■ Any other craft items with interesting colours, shapes or textures.
■ Several glue sticks, large bottle of children's PVA glue.
■ Sellotape.
■ Wide and narrow masking tape.
■ Brass fasteners with blunt ends.
■ Rulers.

- A small selection of junk model materials such as large cardboard boxes, old egg boxes and shoeboxes.
- Coloured pipe-cleaners.
- Tissue/crepe paper.
- Assorted A4 white and coloured paper.
- Assorted A1 sugar paper.
- Card, other shaped paper (including if possible bags of coloured shredding).
- Large bottles of water-soluble paints.
- Finger paints.
- Selection of paint brushes.
- Paint mixers, containers (empty margarine or yogurt pots would be ideal).
- Face paints.
- Playdough in various colours.
- Clay material that dries (preferably not Fymo or other expensive branded products).
- Cutters, shapers, craft tools for the play.
- Possibly aprons (not babyish ones) or old shirts. Otherwise expect very mucky clothes at times.

Spiritual objects

- Small crosses.
- A holding cross.
- Tiny religious pictures, such as icons from a religious bracelet.
- A couple of soft-toy angels.
- Semiprecious stones and gems.
- A couple of small stars.

Natural objects

Choose from these according to the season:
- Feathers.
- Pine cones.
- Sea shells.
- Bark.

- Small branches.
- Leaves.
- Wild flowers.
- Rocks and minerals.

Bits and bobs

Most creative therapy lists have a feminine touch to them. Here are some ideas for bits and bobs from the tool cupboard or 'man shed' that add a little something different and probably won't cost anything extra:

- Spare keys.
- Bolts and nuts.
- Hinges.
- Magnetic cupboard catches.
- Water-pipe holders.
- Small pieces of wood.

In addition, add into the above list toys or small objects that move or make any sort of noise.

Appendix E

Client summary sheet

Name of counsellor:

Client code: Session number: Date:

Type of therapy: Individual child/Family/Therapy group
     Age of child/children:

Brief summary of session, including creative work used:

Supervisor's name and qualifications:
Supervisor's signature: Date:

References and further reading

Allan, John (1988). *Inscapes of the Child's World: Jungian counselling in schools and clinics.* Dallas, Texas: Spring Publications.

American Psychiatric Association (2013). *Diagnostic and Statistical Manual of Mental Disorders, Fifth Edition (DSM-V).* Washington, DC: American Psychiatric Publishing.

Axline, Virginia (1990). *Dibs: In search of self.* London: Penguin. (Original publication 1964.)

Bentovim, Dr Arnold, et al (1991). *Children and Young People as Abusers.* London: National Children's Bureau.

Berne, Eric (1964). *Games People Play.* New York: Grove Press.

Berne, Eric (1966). *Principles of Group Treatment.* London: Oxford University Press.

Berne, Eric (1970). *Sex in Human Loving.* New York: Simon & Schuster.

Berne, Eric (1973). *The Structure and Dynamics of Groups and Organisations.* New York: Ballantine Books/Random House. (Original publication 1963.)

Berne, Eric (1975). *What Do You Say After You Say Hello?* London: Corgi. (Original publication 1972.)

Berne, Eric (1994). *Principles of Group Treatment.* Menlo Park, California: Shea Books. (Original publication 1966).

Campion, Jean (1991). *Counselling Children.* London: Whiting & Birch.

Carey, Lois (1999). *Sandtray Therapy with Children and Families.* Lanham, Maryland: Jason Aronson.

Cattanach, Anne (2002). *The Story So Far: Play therapy narratives.* London: Jessica Kingsley. Original publication 1988.)

Clarkson, Petruska (1992). *Transactional Analysis Psychotherapy: An Integrated Approach.* Abingdon, Oxfordshire: Routledge.

Crossman, Pat (1966). Permission and protection. *Transactional Analysis Bulletin, 5,* 19, pages 152–154.

Daly, John (2005). Workshop presentation.

Day, Christine, & Day, Roger (2014*). Matryoshkas in Therapy: Creative ways to use Rusiian dolls with clients.* Amazon: CreateSpace.

Day, Roger (2004). Being Mad, Being Glad. Oxford: Raintree/Harcourt.

Day, Roger, & Day, Christine (2011). *Body Awareness: 64 bodywork activities for therapy.* Amazon: CreateSpace. (Original publication 2008.)

Day, Roger, & Day, Christine (2012a). *Creative Therapy in the Sand: Using sandtray with clients.* Amazon: CreateSpace.

Day, Roger, & Day, Christine (2012b). *Creative Anger Expression.* Amazon: CreateSpace.

Day, Roger, & Day, Christine (2014). *Stories that Heal: 64 creative visualisations for use in therapy.* Amazon: CreateSpace. (Original publication 2011.)

Day, Roger, & Day, Christine (2015). *Therapeutic Adventure: 64 activities for therapy outdoors.* Amazon: CreateSpace. (Original publication 2008.)

Dunn, Winnie (2007). *Living Sensationally: Understanding your senses.* Jessica Kingsley Publishers.

Egan, Gerard (2013). *The Skilled Helper: A problem-management and opportunity-development approach to helping.* Belmont, California: Wadsworth Publishing. (Originally published 1975.)

English, Fanita (1971). The substitution factor: Rackets and real feelings. *Transactional Analysis Journal, 1,* 4, October 1971, pages 225-230.

English, Fanita (1975). The Three-cornered contract. *Transactional Analysis Bulletin, 5,* 4, page 383, October 1975.

Freeman, Harry, Newland, Lisa, & Coyl, Diana (2010). New directions in father attachment. *Early Child Development and Care 180 (1-2),* pages 1-8, January 2010.

Frick, Paul, Barry, Christopher, and Kamphaus, Randy (1996). *Clinical Assessment of Child and Adolescent Behaviour.* London: Springer Publishing.

Gaudas, Gudrun (2017). www.therapeuticpuppetry.com/THERAPEUTIC-PUPPETRY/

Gladwell, Malcolm (2005). *Blink: The power of thinking without thinking.* London: Penguin Books.

Goodman Robert (1997). The Strengths and Difficulties Questionnaire: A research note. *Journal of Child Psychology and Psychiatry, 38,* pages 581-586.

Goulding & Goulding (1976). Injunctions, decisions and redecisions. *Transactional Analysis Journal, 6,* 1, pages 41-48.

Hadari, Farryl, 2017.
http://www.speakingpuppetry.com/therapy.php

Herman, Judith (2015). *Trauma and Recovery: The aftermath of violence – from domestic abuse to political terror.* New York: Basic Books. (Original publication 1992.)

HM Government (2015). *Working Together to Safeguard Children.* London:
https://www.gov.uk/government/uploads/system/uploads/attachment_data/file/592101/Working_Together_to_Safeguard_Children_20170213.pdf

Illsley-Clarke, Jean (1998). *Self-Esteem: A family affair.* Center City, Minnesota, 1998. (Original publication 1978.)

James, Cathy (2015). https://nurturestore.co.uk

Jennings, Sue (2017). http://www.suejennings.com/epr.html

Johnson, Toni (1999). *Understanding Your Child's Sexual Behaviour.* Oakland, California: New Harbinger Publications.

Justice, Rita, & Blair (1975). Transactional analysis work with child abuse. *Transactional Analysis Journal, 5,* 1, January 1975.

Kellogg, Rhoda (1970). *Analysing Children's Drawings.* Houston, Texas: Mayfield Publishing.

Kranowitz, Carol (1998). *The Out-of-Sync Child.* New York: Penguin.

Kranowitz, Carol (2006). *Out-of-Sync Child has Fun: Activities for kids with sensory processing disorder.* New York: Perigree/Penguin. (Original publication 2003.)

Laban, Rudolph von (1966). *The Language of Movement.* London: Macdonald and Evans.

Laban, Rudolph von (2011). *The Mastery of Movement.* Alton, Hampshire: Dance Books Ltd. (Original work published in 1950.)

Leben, Norma (2000). *Directive Group Play Therapy: 60 structured games for the treatment of ADHD, low self-esteem and traumatised children.* Pflugerville, Texas: Morning Glory Treatment Centre for Children.

Lee, Adrienne (1996). Workshop presentation, Kegworth, Nottinghamshire.

Levin Fox, Shoshana (2005). Workshop presentation, University of East Sussex. Website: http://gethelpisrael.com/therapist/dr-shoshana-levin-fox/

Levin-Landheer, Pam (1988). *Becoming the Way We Are: An introduction to personal development in recovery and in life.* Deerfield Beach, Florida: Health Communications. (Original publication 1975.)

Levin-Landheer, Pam (1982). The cycle of development. *Transactional Analysis Journal, 12,* 2, April 1982, pages 129-139.

Malchiodi, Cathy (2001). *Trauma and loss: Research and interventions, 1, 1,* 2001. Published by the National Institute for Trauma and Loss in Children.

Mills, Joyce C, & Crowley, Richard J (1989). *Cartoon Magic: How to help children discover their rainbows within.* New York: Magination (Brunner/Mazel).

Morris, Don (1999). The power balance in abuse. *ITA Conference Papers,* April 1999.

Mosby (2017). *Mosby's Medical Dictionary 10e.* St Louis, Missouri: Elsevier. (Original publication 1982.)

Napper, Rosemary, & Newton, Trudi (2000). *Tactics: Transactional Analysis Concepts for All Trainers, Teachers and Tutors.* Oxford: TA Resources.

Niolon, Dr Richard (2003). http://www.psychpage.com/ Some of the same material is repeated in: http://www.intelligentietesten.com/house_tree_person_drawings.htm

Rubin, Kenneth (1989). *The Play Observation Scale.* Waterloo, Ontario: University of Waterloo.

Schlippe, Arist von, & Schweitzer, Jochen (1998). *Lehrbuch der Systemischen Therapie und Beratung.* (Göttingen: Vandenhoeck & Ruprecht).

Schwarcz, Ben (2017). www.alternativedepressiontherapy.com/drumming-therapy.html

Souter-Anderson, Lynne (2015). *Making Meaning: Clay therapy with children and adolescents.* Buckingham: Hinton House Publishers.

Steele, Bob (1997). *Draw Me a Story: An illustrated exploration of drawing as pre- and post-literate language.* Winnipeg, Manitoba: Peguis Publishers.

Steiner, Claude (1968). Transactional analysis as a treatment philosophy.
Transactional Analysis Bulletin, 7, 27, pages 61–64.

Steiner, Claude (1999). *Achieving Emotional Literacy.* London: Bloomsbury.

Steiner, Claude (2003). *Emotional Literacy: Intelligence of the heart.* http://emotional-literacy-training.com/wp-content/uploads/2015/09/Steiner-Emotional-Literacy.pdf

Stewart, Ian, & Joines, Vann (1987). *TA Today: A new introduction to transactional analysis.* Nottingham: Lifespace Publishing.

Stewart, Ian (1996). *Developing Transactional Analysis Counselling.* London: Sage Publications.

Stewart, Ian (2002). Workshop notes on leading a visualisation. Kegworth, Nottinghamshire.

Sunderland, Margot (1997). *Draw on Your Emotions.* Abingdon, Oxford: Routledge.

Sunniebunniezz (2017). http://www.sunniebunniezz.com/puppetry/puphisto.htm

Supple, Clifford (2004). Working with traumatised children. *ITA Conference Papers,* April 2004, pages 92-102.

Taylor de Faoite, Aideen, editor (2011). *Narrative Play Therapy: Theory and practice.* London: Jessica Kingsley Publishers.

Thurow, Jean. (1989) Interactional squiggle drawings with children: An illustration of the therapeutic change process. *The Focusing Folio, 8, 4,* pages 149-186.

Tuckman, Bruce (1965). Developmental sequence in small groups. *Psychological Bulletin, 63* (6), pages 384-399.

Tudor, Keith, editor (2007). *The Adult is Parent to the Child: Transactional analysis with children and young people.* Lyme Regis, Dorset: Russell House Publishing.

University of Warwick, 2017. Learning Outcomes. https://warwick.ac.uk/fac/cross_fac/complexity/study/msc_and_phd/co901/learningoutcomes/

Wells, H G (2004). *Floor Games: A father's account of play and its legacy of healing.* Cloverdale, California: Temenos Press. (Original publication 1912.)

White, Tony (1997). Symbiosis and attachment hunger. *Transactional Analysis Journal, 27,* 4, pages 300-304.

Winnicott, Donald (1960). The theory of the parent-child relationship*. International Journal of Psychoanalysis, 41,* pages 585-595.

Winnicott, Donald (1971). *Therapeutic consultations in child psychiatry.* New York: Basic Books.

Yasenik, Lorri, & Gardner, Ken 2012). *Play Therapy Dimensions Model: A decision-making guide for integrative play therapists.* London: Jessica Kingsley. (Original publication 2004.)

Printed in Great Britain
by Amazon